Love in the Tempest of History

A French Resistance Story

Aude Yung–de Prévaux

Translated from the French by Barbara Wright

THE FREE PRESS

New York   London   Toronto   Sydney   Singapore

THE FREE PRESS
A Division of Simon & Schuster, Inc.
1230 Avenue of the Americas
New York, NY 10020

First published in Great Britain 2000
Originally published as *Un amour dans la tempête de l'histoire,*
1999 by Editions du Feélin, Paris

Designed by Lauren Simonetti

Manufactured in the United States of America

1 3 5 7 9 10 8 6 4 2

Library of Congress Cataloging-in-Publication Data
Yung-de Prévaux, Aude.
[Amour dans la tempête de l'histoire. English]
Love in the tempest of history: a French Resistance story /
Aude Yung-de Prévaux; translated from the French by Barbara Wright.
p. cm.
Published in Great Britain under title: Jacques and Lotka.
Includes bibliographical references.
1. Trolley de Prévaux, Jacques, 1888–1944. 2. Prévaux, Lotka de, d. 1944. 3. World War,
1939–1945—Underground movements—France. 4. Guerrillas—France—Biography. I. Title.
D802.F8 Y8613 2000
904.53'44—dc21   00-052805
ISBN 0-7432-0194-9

Resistance fighters, you who were killed in the maquis or executed by firing squad, all of you who with your last breath shouted aloud the name of France, you are the men and women who exalted courage, sanctified effort, invented resolution. You took the lead at the head of the immense, magnificent cohort of the sons and daughters of France who, through their suffering, bore witness to her greatness.

GENERAL CHARLES DE GAULLE, Preface to
Mémorial des compagnons de la Libération

Heroes—human beings who refuse to be subjugated.

JEAN GIONO

CONTENTS

Acknowledgments   *ix*

Prologue   1

PART I: JACQUES

1. The Would-be Buccaneer   9
2. The War Years   18
3. Airship Pilot   28
4. Rank and Respectability   35
5. Naval Attaché in Berlin   44
6. On the China Seas   54

PART II: LOTKA

7. From Jaroslaw to Vionnet   67
8. Conquest by Correspondence   78
9. Rochefort   85
10. A Double Life   90
11. On the *Duguay-Trouin*   98
12. Force X in Alexandria   110

PART III: VOX AND KALO

13. In the Maritime Court   123
14. Commitment   131

15. F2—A Franco-Polish Network   136
16. The Subterfuge   141
17. A Simple Informer   151
18. Fighting in the Shadows   160
19. The Arrest of the Leitners   167
20. Vox in Danger   172
21. Montluc   178

Afterword   *185*
Jacques de Prévaux's Military Career   *189*
Principal Decorations and Awards   *193*
Sources   *199*

ACKNOWLEDGMENTS

This book would never have been either started or finished without the support of Admiral Michel Debray. I would also like to thank him for having accepted the tedious task of reading it in draft form and correcting the naval terms. Captain Robert Feuilloy was good enough to do the same in the domain of naval aviation, and I would like to thank him for having guided my research among the documents on the beginnings of the Naval Air Services.

The indulgent help and encouragement of Jean-Louis Crémieux-Brilhac were invaluable to me.

Rear Admiral Jean Kessler made me extremely welcome, both when he was head of the Service historique de la Marine and later, as did Mme. René-Bazin at the National Archives. Their advice and help were of the greatest use to me.

I owe to the historian Pascal Mercier my knowledge of the role my father played with Pierre Viénot in the Franco-German Committee.

My thanks to all my parents' former companions, colleagues and comrades-in-arms for having received me and agreed to search their memories and share their recollections with me: Captain Borderies, Eva Bringué-Tournier, Admiral de Brossard, Rear Admiral Chevillotte, Captain Georges Debat, Natacha Duché, Colonel Pierre Fourcaud, Dr Jean Godeau, Gaston Havard, Daniéla Jeanson, Willy Leitner, Stanislas Lucki, Jacques Lévy-

Rueff, Roland de Margerie, Camille Migaud, Colonel Paillole, Mathilde Pascalis, Guy Simon, Léon Sliwinski, Michel Trolley de Prévaux, and Mme. Vastenbeerghe.

I am particularly grateful to Mathilde Pascalis and her son Eric, who for nearly fifty years faithfully preserved my parents' letters.

And finally, thank you to my family and friends for having shown so much patience and understanding during the gestation of this book.

Love in the Tempest of History

Prologue

I was twenty-three when, by pure chance, I discovered who I really was. My parents, it seemed, were not the elderly couple who had brought me up. This was a momentous revelation in itself, the sort that uproots you from a comfortable legacy of provincial grandparents and holidays spent in the shadow of country churches. The small events of a happy childhood take on a different light. You are no longer who you used to be. Your whole life story must be rewritten.

It was 1966 and I was a student in Paris. That year I was writing a dissertation on "Cathar Dualism," and spending every day at the Bibliothèque Nationale deciphering mountains of dusty folios. The dull murmur rising from the reading room, the faint light of the green lamps while the Paris sky above the high glass roof was slowly darkening, the musty smell of the ancient books, all contributed to the contemplative atmosphere, from which I used to emerge dazed and reeling. My supervisor was somewhat indifferent to the progress of my thesis: he occasionally invited me to a tearoom in the Latin Quarter where, over cream puffs, he discoursed on nothingness, or on the devil and the stake at Montségur, while squeezing my knee.

One afternoon I was writing my name in block capitals on one of the green slips you used to have to complete to order the books you wanted, when I noticed that the elderly man on my right was looking at what I was writing.

"Forgive me for asking, but aren't you the daughter of Admiral Trolley de Prévaux?"

He spoke in a rasping voice that couldn't manage a whisper. The reader sitting opposite me looked up, and I was horribly embarrassed. Even though his question was absurd, I thought it better to answer this courteous man and so avoid further interrogation. My father, who had been dead for ten years, was indeed a military man, but a general. Maybe my interlocutor had confused equivalent ranks? However, I was categorical: there had never been an admiral in my family. But I would mention it to my mother, perhaps she would know. . . .

He interrupted me, insisting as if he was more and more sure that he was right: "That name and that Christian name—it can only be you. And you are so like poor Lotka. . . . You *were* born in Nice in June 1943? You see! But of course, your adoptive parents hid the truth from you. I remember now. We weren't allowed to see you. Because of the tragedy. My poor child—"

He was overcome, he could no longer manage to keep his voice down. The people around us were furiously muttering "Shh, shh." I had turned pale. I must have stammered some stupid question and asked what had happened, because with a handful of sentences he had shattered my peaceful world.

"My poor child! Your parents were heroes. They were in the Resistance, they were killed by the Germans. You were only a baby. . . . Your mother was Jewish, Polish I think. She was very beautiful, much younger than your father, who was an admiral. *Voilà.*"

Voilà. I don't know what happened next. When I emerged from the stupor his words had plunged me into, he had gone. The reading room had calmed down. It took me some time to do the same.

I was going to have to find a new identity. At first, you don't even need any details. A handful of fragments—heroes of the Resistance, an admiral, a Jewess, Poland—are enough to start you dreaming and imagining links between what you are and what you thought you were. When you have carefully digested and assimilated them, then you can begin to ask questions.

Micheline, my (adoptive) mother, had seemed relieved that I had discovered the truth and wasn't bothered by the blunt way it had been broken to me. Obliged to pronounce the words that for twenty-two years she hadn't had the strength to utter—that I wasn't her daughter—she confined herself to the strict terms of my civil status. According to her, she knew nothing about these parents I had just discovered. She took refuge in the war years—the uncertainties, the difficulties in communication, the family's disapproval of her marriage, late in life, to François, the brother of my father the admiral.

Micheline considered that the fact of my adoption implied the abolition of my past, and she had given everyone strict instructions to say nothing. Her orders had been scrupulously followed by the very bourgeois Trolley de Prévaux family, which, as I was to discover later, had been scandalized by various episodes in my father's life and by my mother's origins. So the secret was kept for twenty-two years. When she had tried to run this blockade, my maternal aunt had been declared persona non grata and, along with her, my entire Polish ancestry. The nurse who had taken me in after my parents' arrest was unceremoniously sent back to her village, and her letters innocently asking for news of me went unanswered. When I tried to find out what sort of life my parents had lived, the whole family seemed to be suffering from amnesia. I did manage to discover that my Polish godfather knew more. He was living in Morocco and I hardly knew him but he was still looking after some of my father's belongings, which had been entrusted to him, and was waiting for permission to send them to me.

My father's trunks duly arrived from Morocco. They invaded the drawing room, taking over what was left of the space between the Louis XV chairs and the divan I used as a bed. They were two solid, iron-bound wooden chests, each lined with a waterproof metal sheet, showing signs of the various transshipments they had undergone, and of the frequent typhoons in the China seas on which they had sailed for so many years. On a yellowed label, I could make out the beautifully written name of my father, Captain Jacques de Prévaux, and also the name of the ship he commanded, the *Duguay-Trouin.*

These trunks, now run aground on the carpet, must surely have retained the smell of the sea. I imagined I could detect a whiff of iodine and salt, the spicy remains of an Asiatic voyage, traces of opium, and even the lingering odor of the rum on which the crew, down in the hold, must have become intoxicated during their ritual drinking sessions while, in his noble white uniform, accompanied by colonial beauties, the captain— my father!—strolled along the Shanghai *Bund.* But the chests no longer smelled of anything. They had been gathering dust for a quarter of a century in an office in Casablanca, waiting to be sent to me when finally I had been told the truth about my lineage.

Opened with trembling hands, at first all that the trunks revealed, tucked into the middle of piles of starched linen, was a collection of old deckle-edged photographs, official navy papers, school exercise books, quantities of books and manuscripts, and a bundle of letters tied with a ribbon, a bewildering jumble. I went straight to the photos and scattered them impatiently. I could not wait to see my father's face, to discover my mother. . . . But they remained enigmatic, and it was unbearable. Micheline was unable to answer my questions. Of all these smiling couples, which were my parents? Of all those officers lined up on the poop deck facing the photographer, which one is my father? Is he this one, or perhaps that one, over there? That woman leaning over a cot—is she my mother, and is that me in her arms? What were they like, who were they? Who was I?

I decided then that this story didn't concern me, that it was before my time. But once opened, the trunks weren't going to allow themselves to be shut up again so easily. It was not possible to put everything neatly back, to shut the lids and banish them to the attic. There was always something that stuck out and refused to be locked away: the Tibetan Book of the Dead and the books of Hindu philosophy, subjects in which I had long been passionately interested; the false papers with which a young woman had crossed the border, hiding in her handbag documents to be sent to London; the photo of a baby in the arms of the same radiant young woman; the prayer shawl, the books in Hebrew; the service record book, with its long, eulogistic list of various postings; the words of love that seemed to emanate from the letters even before I had dared untie the packets.

I had to put a name to these faces, and faces to my unknown parents. To find people who had witnessed their lives—after such a long time, very few were left—and get them to tell me everything they remembered. To bury myself in the archives of the Naval Records Department and search the National Archives. To go back to the Bibliothèque Nationale and look for their names in the files. To try to discover why the navy, which had given France so few resisters, had done so little to honor the name of this particular admiral. And above all, I had to read, with burning cheeks, their letters, thousands of letters, notes, telegrams, a cornucopia that, as if by a miracle, had made its way to me by an improbable series of events and suddenly overflowed at my feet.

And, gradually, my parents emerged from the shadows, and their romantic, tragic life pieced itself together. The outline of an exceptional young man began to take shape. A brilliant officer in the French Navy who disobeyed his superiors' orders and went over to the Resistance in 1941; an aristocrat from an ultra-Catholic background who rejected his family's moral code,

PART I

JACQUES

1
THE WOULD-BE BUCCANEER

On the poop deck of the torpedo boat *Chasseur,* a sailor was looking up at the stars, dreaming. He wore his uniform with distinction, but he was extremely thin. He looked ill and exhausted, his burning eyes seeming to take up the whole of his face. A dog-eared book stuck out of the pocket of his pea jacket. The sight of the massive figure of the captain suddenly emerging from the shadows recalled him to duty. Quickly thrusting the book deep into his pocket, Sub-Lieutenant de Prévaux stood to attention, reeled off a few details of the distance they had covered, the present position of the ship and the course they had followed, and anxiously awaited further instructions. There were none. Reassured, after a final salute he returned to his reverie. His hands, which were very beautiful, began to move toward his pocket. If he dared, he would bring out the book and finish it. It was a calm night, the *Chasseur* seemed to be quite alone, sailing over a smooth, sparkling sea, and the Cyclades were still a good few nautical miles off to the northeast.

Jacques de Prévaux loved the night watches, when he could imagine he was alone in the world, surrounded by the familiar dark shapes of the navigational instruments, lulled by the slight vibration of the gray metal plating. Solitude was his element. He could let his thoughts wander, dream of his romances in his last ports of call, think of what he was soon going to write in his diary, or even surreptitiously read a few pages of the book he always had with him, without attracting the gibes of the other members of the watch, who regarded him as an intellectual. If he hadn't been so reserved he would have shut them up, but what could he say to them? It was true that he was at ease only with books; human contacts frightened him. When anyone approached him he would flinch; he had to make a real effort to sit down with others at mealtimes. He loathed the promiscuity and boisterous fraternity of the wardrooms, yet despised himself for not being able to join in. But he knew this was also a part of the navy, and every day he spent at sea confirmed him in the belief that the navy was his true vocation. His reticence prevented him from revealing his romantic soul, but he needed a friend and imagined that no one but his captain was capable of understanding him. He confided his doubts to his diary, although he believed them unworthy of a future naval officer: "Was I right to choose this career? Alas! I really do believe I am ugly! And lazy, what's more; I haven't read a line for two days, and not only because I've been ill." Yet he felt sure that he had been called to an exceptional destiny.

A few lights from Mílos were beginning to appear. The sub-lieutenant reluctantly abandoned his contemplation of the Greek sky, which had led him to think about the Cretan philosophers and the harmony they read into the arrangement of the stars. The harmony was still there, for all eternity, serene and peaceful. And yet, over on the Marne, the same stars were shining down on fighting men half-buried in the trenches, on corpses engulfed in mud, on shell holes. At that time—autumn 1914—Jacques de Prévaux was waging war by patrolling the waters off the mythically named Greek islands. After a last despairing look at the splendor of the night, he returned with a sigh to the business of changing course, for which he had to give the order.

* * *

Jacques de Prévaux had no reason to doubt his naval vocation. When he joined the *Chasseur* his work had already been assessed in flattering terms. With his first postings he had come to the attention of his superiors, who saw him as an "astonishingly gifted" officer and had observed his sangfroid, his qualities as a man of the world (an important asset in the eyes of the aristocratic milieu of the French Navy), his ability to assimilate knowledge and his exceptional intelligence, all of which boded well for a brilliant career. The officers in charge of both his squadron and his division were full of praise for him: "Shows remarkable promise. He seems to have the makings of an officer with a great future."

And yet his family traditions did not destine him for a military career, and his instructors at the Naval College, where he came third out of the forty-eight entrants, deplored the fact that he "lacked the military spirit," although they recognized the laudable efforts he made to acquire it. The Trolley de Prévaux were an ancient Norman family of lawyers, which in March 1586 received their letters patent of nobility from King Henri III. The family genealogy, which Jacques was sometimes allowed to examine, lists an abundance of magistrates, bailiffs and judges. No soldiers at all, unless Joan of Arc could be counted among their ancestors—a certain Marie-Madeleine, a descendant of the older brother of the Maid of Orleans, is said to have married, in 1733, Pierre Trolley de Prévaux, esquire, bodyguard to the king.

Jacques' more recent ancestors were outstanding members of the austere legal profession. His great-uncle Jacques was a professor of law at the University of Caen, and the famous author of *A Treatise on the Administrative Hierarchy* in five volumes. His maternal grandfather, Amédée de Margerie, the dean of the arts faculty in the Catholic University of Lille and the founder of the Catholic University of Nancy, was the family's paragon in all moral and cultural matters. He left a large number of imperishable works, including *On the Family: Lessons in Moral Philosophy*. As for Jacques' father, Alfred—who insisted on using his whole surname, whereas Jacques was content to be just Jacques de Prévaux—had for forty-five years occupied the chair of commercial law at the Catholic University of Lille. At his funeral in 1921 he was celebrated as "a courteous, softly spoken, urbane, hospitable man who led a peaceful, well-ordered life. . . . All the leisure his professional and family duties allowed him he devoted to charitable works, which he carried out with the simplicity of a man of an earlier era." This decidedly exemplary family seems to have been dedicated to religion. Jacques' father was a tertiary of Saint Francis of Assisi and a Knight of the Order of Saint Gregory the Great; his three aunts Sidonie, Bertille and Ernestine entered a convent in the strictest of all monastic orders, the Carmelites.

Jacques and his two surviving brothers—three others died in infancy—were brought up to have rigid respect for the most traditional moral principles. Inconsolable after the death of his wife, their father, always of a severe nature, withdrew into a life of penitence and solitude. Jacques spent his childhood in a house in mourning, where silence was expected and laughter condemned as an outrage to the soul of his dead mother. Later, any communication between the father and his sons was limited to routine moral exhortations and curt reports on the management of the family monies, which were modest. Jacques was eleven when his mother died. The only tenderness in this masculine world disappeared with her and he suffered profoundly from his father's inability to express paternal love.

When he was sent to school at Saint-Joseph's in Lille, he was a charming little boy with a direct, honest gaze, a determined, almost cheeky, air and was expert at shooting birds out of their nests with his catapult. He found the atmosphere at the Jesuit school as pained as it was at home. Quite simply, he seemed to fade away. Studies and penitence ruled the days. Solitude was highly thought of, and budding friendships were carefully monitored so that they could be broken before they developed dangerously. His teachers appreciated this hardworking, obedient pupil. He received top marks and the worst thing they could reproach him with was a suspect penchant for literature. They saw his respect for discipline as submission, his adolescent reserved character as good behavior, his interest in theology as piety, never imagining either his desire for the absolute or the force of a personality that was struggling to survive the leveling process intact.

This miserable childhood gave Jacques a melancholy character. Convinced that nobody understood him, he withdrew into himself and found joy only in dreams and in books. He certainly recognized his aspirations towards a different life from that of his virtuous family, but could only conceive of it as being elsewhere, somewhere very far away from Lille.

Jacques decided to join the navy. With no knowledge of the sea beyond the windy Flanders beaches where he was sometimes taken to play, he suddenly began to dream of the infinity of the oceans and of big ships weighing anchor. To go to sea, to escape without seeming to be running away.

"I'm a Norman, the son of buccaneers," de Prévaux proclaimed, taking a few liberties with his genealogy. Skipping several generations of tranquil Normans, he had discovered a remote Breton ancestor said to have been a pirate in Martinique. The fact that Nicolas Fèbvrier de Mésaillet had been killed in 1732 during an expedition sent to St. Lucia to crush some mutineers made no difference; he passed for a freebooter. And in Jacques' own mutiny against a too-respectable family, he believed he had Creole blood—which, after all, was not impossible. To give himself an ancestry to suit his tastes, he picked out this pirate, and fashioned himself a line of descent worthy of what he imagined to be his destiny. Jacques was reborn. He could finally create himself.

During the dreary boarding school evenings with the Jesuits, Jacques would see himself voyaging far away from Lille. In the wake of the corsair, his ancestor, he would drift in a daze toward his imagined destiny, fantasizing about the fertility and exuberance of the Caribbean. Above all, he would picture the sea, the ports full of clamor and strange smells, the ships, their holds crammed with booty, changing course with a great flapping of sails and then scudding off under the skilled command of a daredevil captain.... When, at twenty, he reached the West Indies for the first time, he was to recognize those islands "which our childhood dreams people with laughing, fantastic images." No doubt he scribbled sketches of ships in the margins of his school exercise books. Then—since he had been taught that whatever he did he must do well—he learned by heart the name of every piece of rigging and every sail, down to the smallest possible bit of rope.

He was ready to go to sea, to turn his back forever on crass provincial life, his stifling milieu, his taciturn father and his overregulated existence. To go to sea, but not as an ordinary seaman. Given his social standing and his excellent school reports, it had to be the Naval College. His family was disconcerted by this bizarre vocation but, all things considered, they thought it preferable to literature.

After a year at the Naval College, Jacques had his first experience of navigation. As excited as a group of schoolboys going on holiday, his class set off for two months on board the training cruiser *Bougainville*. The apprenticeship to life at sea is hard. At first the young aristocrat was upset by the lack of comfort. Water was rationed, he had to get used to having dirty hands and wearing filthy clothes, and the hammocks were so close together that in a heavy swell the sleeping men would bump into one another. He became familiar with the unpleasant regular jobs that had to be done: the grueling watches in the inferno of the boiler room, the struggle at the capstan with two anchor chains that had become entangled during the night, the never-ending maneuvers that sent a watch to set up the sails only to be told to furl them an hour later.

Luckily, during the months spent together in Brest, the traditions of the Naval College and the authority of the chain of command had caused the novice crew to bond. Like the other boys who were not yet twenty, Jacques went through all the chaotic exercises with childish gaiety. Far outside the school walls, and for the first time away from his family, he found great enjoyment in a few simple pleasures: managing to track down some *petits-beurre* for his tea, going ashore with his gang of shipmates in the Bay of Morlaix, where they were proud of frightening the peaceful natives with their bizarre clothes and rowdy behavior, singing on the fo'c'sle in the evenings to the accompaniment of an old accordion, smoking his pipe with the gravity of his elders. But nothing equaled the experience of his first storm in the Shetlands, where the *Bougainville* was hove to.

The following year Jacques left the college and embarked with the midshipmen of his year on the training ship *Duguay-Trouin* on a cruise around the world. There they laboriously applied the techniques studied on land. They learned the rudiments of diplomacy, discovered other worlds, and enjoyed themselves. Jacques was twenty, and felt free for the first time. The discipline, for which his whole education had prepared him, did not weigh too heavily on him. On the contrary, he was intoxicated with space, and with so many new things. It was as if an enormous breath of fresh air from the high seas were suddenly blowing through his confined spirit.

Every sailor who has experienced the customary training cruise retains fabulous memories of it. Interested in everything, Jacques opened his eyes wide to the world and, with his companions, marveled at the delicacy of the lace in Malta, amused himself bargaining for cigars in Havana or ebony walking sticks in Dakar, made gentle fun of the bellboy uniforms of the Mexican armies and of the propensity of the Norwegians to wolf down vast quantities of hors d'oeuvres, and admired the haughty carriage of the ladies of Seville.

He allowed himself to be caught up in the whirl of the carefree, pleasure-loving midshipmen, who rushed from receptions at the yacht club to balls given in their honor, where they danced all night long with society girls. At every port of call they would engage in romances in every language and, on their departure, would laugh as they threw ribbons in the colors of the *Duguay-Trouin* down to the boatloads of beauties come to blow good-bye kisses to their dancing partners of a single evening.

Certainly, Jacques was always prepared to come down to earth and join in the wild outings of the members of the watch, but gradually he began to prefer studious visits to churches, museums, concerts and the peace of the bridge, where he could read and think. He also spent a lot of time writing the reports that he had to give the captain at each port of call. These were in his best handwriting and decorated with the naïve postcards of yesteryear. At first he was very proud of his reports, and of the captain's assessment of them: "Well written . . . correct style and a pleasure to read. . . . Nice turns of phrase." But when one of his reports included "We had a little rain," he was cut to the quick by a contemptuous comment written in red ink in the margin: "You talk like an infantryman." Then he discovered that it wasn't enough to have style. His pride had been wounded, and he decided to make it a point of honor to hand in reports that were both precise and literary, because he wanted to become a naval officer. He was now quite sure that that was what he was made for. He had been delighted to discover that the sea he had so often dreamt of had kept its promises, that going to sea was all he had wished for. Seen from Lille or Lambersart, however, this didn't appear so obvious.

In his reports, Jacques describes how, when his ship was being fitted out in Brest on 10 October 1908, he experienced "the emotion of a fanatical enthusiast who couldn't wait to set sail," the joy and surprises of his first voyage, on a real oceangoing vessel, the joy of the blue sea, of the speeding white *Duguay,* of his first stripe, of his growing freedom after the stringency of the *Borda,* the training ship anchored in Brest. He savored his first night watch, his first attempts at familiarizing himself with the stars, and his first Atlantic crossing—from the Canary Islands to Guadeloupe. At last he was finally at sea, where he felt so much at ease.

> I wish I could put into words all of the impression of perfect peace of mind and supreme tranquillity of spirit that I felt during those first twelve days on that uniformly blue, calm sea, on which the wake of our big white boat was barely perceptible. The vastness of the ocean extends your horizons and elevates your whole being; and in that total monotony, the tiniest little thing—the sun rising with its band of golden clouds, the full moon one evening with its blue reflections shining on the phosphorescent water, one star brighter than all the rest, a sailing ship on the horizon—that's all you need for your imagination to give itself up to infinite reveries.

He really couldn't understand the men who were pining for their home ports and dreaming about the return journey. Separation didn't bother him, and he didn't see his days at sea as days of waiting. Nautical life was indeed his vocation.

When he left the training school at twenty-one, de Prévaux was one of the hopes of the navy. They saw him as the ideal midshipman—serious, gentlemanly, from an aristocratic family—with the makings of an officer, and one of the very best.

A few years later, everything seemed lost.

2
THE WAR YEARS

De Prévaux was given his first posting in 1910, to the battleship *Charlemagne* based in Toulon, which from then on was his home port. He was assigned to the main armament and fire-control teams. Nothing very exciting. He applied himself, though, worked hard and was highly thought of by his superiors. He was a good, conscientious student who made it a point of honor to do well. His commander, Captain Morier, saw him as a thoughtful, shy young man who had yet to develop a deep liking for the naval life.

Jacques hadn't imagined that the assignment would keep him constantly in dock, and he found the tedious work a strain. After the peregrinations of the *Duguay-Trouin* and the intoxication of sailing the high seas, life in port seemed very dull. Going ashore on a spree with sailors held no appeal for him. He still had no friends, and suffered in his solitude. What was the good of reading so many books if you couldn't share your feelings about them with anyone?

Finally, Jacques got to know Jean Roulier. This young midshipman, three years younger than Jacques, was a poet. Tall, handsome and fearless, with an ironic smile perpetually on his lips, Roulier had all the qualities necessary to make a success of life. He was later one of the ten first pilots in the navy, designed the plans for a combat seaplane that could reach 130 kilometers an hour, and during the war fought with the bomber squadrons. Jacques was fascinated by his daredevil character. Through him he lived the adventure of the pioneer of naval aviation, and he later decided to follow his younger friend's example and join the Naval Air Service. Jean Roulier was killed six years later, on August 15, 1916, in aerial combat over Trieste. An Austrian fighter grazed his brand-new seaplane while he was bombing enemy positions. His friend Gabriele d'Annunzio, himself wounded in the eye a few days later, delivered a moving oration at his military funeral in Venice. "He died in the splendor of the daylight, he fell into the sea like a light, like a diurnal meteorite, and his noble blood has left its mark on the pure Italian sky."

At Toulon, the two young men discovered that they had many things in common—a love of poetry, a feeling of being misunderstood by their families, a determination to break with their conventional backgrounds, and a liking for endless discussions on the meaning of life and other subjects prudently sidestepped by their professors at the Naval College. Claiming to be disillusioned, each was actually as romantic as the other, although Jean showed more practical sense and was more of a hedonist than Jacques. Roulier's family was wealthy, and he had rented an apartment in rue Victor-Clappier, which he lent to his friends on condition that they respected certain strict rules. The key was more or less at their disposal, provided they never took women there. The landlord was a prude. In what they called their "Chinese cabinet," Jacques and he spent delightful evenings in conversation, stretched out on a wide sofa, while opium pellets sizzled on their needles and the little stove threw a faint light on the wall hangings that Jean, who collected oriental art, had brought back from China. Their only worry was that the fragrant smoke from their pipes might alert their ever-vigilant neighbors. Jean was in love, or rather he was having a passionate and self-destructive affair with a demimondaine who owned an opium den. Henriette, known as The Dragonfly, had a hold on him he couldn't break, although he was ashamed of it. In the end, he took refuge in Paris to free himself from her and from opium. Jacques, on the other hand, only managed to give up the drug much later.

At that time, opium taking was common practice in the navy, which had brought that exotic fashion back from the Far East. A mysterious ritual, abundant literature conferred on it the cachet of spirituality, or at least of refinement. Frenetic smoking went on in the ports—in Toulon in particular, where more than two hundred opium dens were well established and almost respectable—until the military authorities intervened. They were not worried by the possible risk to the smooth running of their ships—which was practically nil—as by the risk of the navy's honor being besmirched by the attention of the press. However, they took action only against recognized addicts. Yet how many naval officers smoked or ate opium? The precedent came from on high, from the officer who, under the pseudonym of Claude Farrère, wrote *Fumée d' opium,* a work that Jacques was to read and reread aboard the *Descartes.* This skilled apologia for the drug conferred a cultural, even religious alibi on opium: it brought peace and understanding. Like so many other young officers, Jacques smoked serenely for many years until he began to see that he was no longer master of himself.

In January 1912, de Prévaux was again at sea. The second-class cruiser *Descartes,* with a crew of four-hundred men, sixteen of whom were officers, was posted to the fishing grounds off Newfoundland and the east coast of America. She was an old ship, launched eighteen years previously, and was not luxurious. Her bridge was cluttered with twenty-four big guns, and all this weaponry made it impossible to hold dancing parties there, to the great regret of the officers.

After the traditional tour of the West Indies, the ship's mission was to watch over French interests in Newfoundland, to protect ten-thousand fishermen, rescue them in case of distress, take the sick or wounded on board and treat them, and possibly evacuate them to hospitals in St. John in Newfoundland, or Sydney in Cape Breton. Finally, she had to patrol the icy waters, looking out, for instance, for illegal lobster fishing. At that time she was the finest boat deployed. Although like all sailors Jacques would have preferred to go to China, he was nevertheless delighted to have returned to the healthy life of the open sea, to navigation, to hot days in the tropics. At first, however, this renewed contact with the sea was difficult. The weather was so bad that it exhausted the seamen and turned the 'tween-decks, wardrooms and cabins into noxious swamps. You were better off on watch on the bridge, exposing your face to the spray, "in the middle of the marvelous concert of the creaking, howling, plaintive voices of the wind, the rigging, the whole groaning, vibrating hull."

De Prévaux was attached to the special section comprising electrical equipment, torpedoes and fire prevention, and was also responsible for the archives covering foreign navies. His commander was Captain Pugliesi-Conti, a caricature of an old sea dog—a big, tall man with a substantial beard and an affable manner, a real father to his crew, who respected and adored him. The captain didn't conceal his disappointment, though: true, de Prévaux was an excellent officer of the watch, he had "a great talent for writing" which would make him a very good staff officer, but he was a bit indolent. In short, "He shows moderate enthusiasm," an elegant way of saying that this young sub-lieutenant, although he had been preceded by a flattering reputation, didn't devote all his energies to the smooth running of the service.

What Jacques did with his energies was to use them for more interesting occupations, reading and writing. Whenever he had a spare moment, on the poop deck or elsewhere, he would whip

a book out of the distended pocket of his pea jacket and become absorbed in reading. He thought of the crossing from Lorient to Dakar as the Gide crossing—*Marshlands* was his
bedside book at that time—and when the *Descartes* was cruising off the Canary Islands it was in the name of Ruskin. After
they'd crossed the line, Montaigne appeared from eight until
midnight, under the stars. Oscar Wilde occupied the journey
from Rio to Belém. Péguy revealed himself from four to eight
in the morning between Havana and Haiti. Then came Shake-
speare, and, farther on, Maurice Barrès. . . . The invisible lines
the *Descartes* traced on the oceans became the itineraries of his
literary discoveries.

His rank entitled him to a cabin, which he immediately filled
with books and reams of paper. When the latter ran out, he
made do with pages torn out of the logbook. The moment he
came off duty he settled down at his typewriter, whose ribbon
soon gave him trouble, and jotted down his thoughts about the
books he'd read and his impressions of the wonderful scenery
he had somehow found time to notice between maneuvers. He
kept two parallel diaries. One was literary, in which he expressed the feelings of "the observer, the aesthete, the artist-er-
rant" he claimed to be. The other, which he called "special," was
reserved for girls and for the unmentionable (opium), his difficulties in finding alternatives for it, his vague intention of
breaking the habit. And then, as an enthusiastic response to
reading Stendhal's Journal, he began to rework his notes and
turn them into a third diary, this one intended to be published.
Also an inveterate letter writer, he hardly slept, and his health
was beginning to suffer from overwork.

When the ship was in port, he cut a swath in the gambling
dens and sailors' cabarets, which he was expected to frequent.
Together with the balls at the French club, the tea parties, cock-
tail parties and other diplomatic chores were all part of a
sailor's life. At that time, the officers of a warship were enter-

tained most lavishly in the towns, suddenly ablaze with tricolor flags, and the local papers devoted page after page to describing the enthusiasm of the inhabitants. The notables who represented the French community—the chamber of commerce, the leagues of friendship, and so on—the ecclesiastical authorities, the consular officials, the local functionaries headed by the mayor, all vied with each other for the honor of inviting the officers of the *Descartes* to sumptuous banquets, where they were plied with champagne. Some ports of call had a special reputation for the quality of their welcome or for the vintage wines they served, so much so that on some occasions the captain, accustomed as he was to carousing, had to make excuses and keep to his bed.

The sublieutenants spent their shore leave in ways that were less strictly diplomatic. De Prévaux teamed up with a few friends from his wardroom to form a bizarre group of bushy-bearded, strapping young sailors among whom this clean-shaven, emaciated young man, with circles under his eyes from lack of sleep, was practically invisible. The gang made it a point of honor to behave with courtesy, to be jovial, gallant, bring flowers, and always be ready to sit down at the piano—in short, to be worthy representatives of France and the navy. This made them popular and won them the confidence of their superiors, so they were able to slip away from official receptions unobtrusively, under the indulgent eye of their admirals. Jacques was not the life and soul of the group, but his sickly appearance made him look interesting. He played Chopin to perfection, and his eyes proved irresistible to the girls.

He would sometimes duck out of these decorous evenings, although there was always plenty to drink, and disappear into some opium den run by the Chinese. Again under its sway, to him opium evoked "cool mats, subdued lamplight, and fine books read with better understanding." The torpor of the West Indies contributed to his drug-influenced inertia, though he preferred to believe himself lazy. He recognized himself in Conrad's character, "who in common with all mariners," when he was not on duty "liked to savor the full charm of absolute irresponsibility," and who "felt he had unlimited aptitudes for doing nothing." It is understandable that his captain should call his enthusiasm "moderate."

Soon, however, work began to impose its own rhythm. At St. Pierre et Miquelon, off Newfoundland, the inspection of the Grand Banks had to be organized, the rounds of the schooners had to be set up. The cold and the ghostly trips in the fog between the icebergs woke him up. He finally felt he had a strong, healthy impression of the job, and yet the exigencies of his work didn't put him off opium, nor prevent him from writing his triple diary. All through the eighteen months the voyage was to last, he tried to reconcile conflicting aspirations and to do everything at once: to perform his demanding, physically exhausting duties on board and at the same time lead an intense intellectual life, while still not cutting himself off from his shipmates' binges and also managing to fall desperately in love with a girl in every port. Quite enough to cause physical and nervous exhaustion.

When the *Descartes* returned to her home port, Jacques was sent to the hospital. He was treated for "tropical anemia" and then spent three months' convalescent leave in Toulon. In fact, he was never really cured, and for the rest of his life he suffered from delicate health and a tendency to anemia.

In 1914 de Prévaux joined a torpedo flotilla of the First Fleet. To start with, he served as second officer on the torpedo boat *Fanfare,* on which he showed what he was capable of and was highly commended. He became ill again, though, and had to be put ashore and readmitted to the hospital.

His new assignment, at the end of August 1914—war had just

been declared—took him to another torpedo boat, the *Chasseur,* where he was both navigating and gunnery officer. His two years of service on the *Chasseur* were torture. In the first place, he was profoundly affected by the war. True, he was not at the front, the mission of his squadron being to escort Serbian convoys in the Greek waters between Mílos and Argostólion, but he suffered from this inaction and did his best to be sent closer to the combat zone. As early as 1915 he asked Jean Roulier, whose aerial exploits filled him with admiration, to sound out his superiors to see whether there was any chance of his being accepted in the Naval Air Service. It was simply out of the question: at this stage of the war, officers could not so easily leave their units. The following year he put in an official request, and it was finally granted a year before the peace.

Jacques' health continued to deteriorate. He was cured neither of opium nor of anemia and became frighteningly thin. He couldn't sleep, yet was so tired that he could hardly stay on his feet when on duty. He even suffered from blackouts. His commander, Captain Kerboul, finally became worried and sought the cause of this permanent exhaustion. Rumors began to spread and, worse, comments in his file began to suggest that de Prévaux might be taking drugs.

Eventually, Jacques got back on his feet. He was ashamed of himself and thought he could read contempt in his superiors' eyes. He realized sadly that he hardly read anymore, and wrote even less. He was also cut to the quick by the remonstrations of the two friends he thought of as brothers. Jean Roulier, who knew what smoking opium meant, had realized why Jacques looked so ill and was so irritable. He rebuked him, and begged him to "give up those frightful poisons completely." Roland de Margerie, his first cousin, made himself the spokesman of the horror-stricken family: "When they saw you looking so dreadful, they had no hesitation in attributing it to drugs."

Roland, who was ten years younger than Jacques, kept up a literary and sentimental correspondence with him. This brilliant young man, destined by his gifts and by his family connections for a great diplomatic career, had been dazzled by his older cousin. In his eyes, Jacques represented an intense life of action, which he himself only knew through books. When he was fifteen, he wrote to him: "The kind of total mental confusion I felt after I saw you for the first time is a sign of my interest in you." Roland was later to play the same part with Jacques as Roulier had done, that of the talented, admiring younger man, of the affectionate brother, for whom the intellectual bond wiped out the difference in age. Their letters are real literary chronicles. Roland devoured whole libraries, at the rate of two books a day, and confessed—he was seventeen—that he was "so addled with literature" that he could no longer "really feel anything at all," that it made him feel "rather old to have thought all these feelings without ever having experienced them."

By May 1916, Jacques had regained full possession of his faculties, so much so that the new captain of the *Chasseur* couldn't make head or tail of the bad report handed on to him from his predecessor. When de Prévaux was transferred to the gunboat *Diligente,* which was attached to the division patrolling the eastern Mediterranean, his reports were once again written in the glowing terms of earlier days. He was second officer, and found it a joy to serve on this brand-new vessel, with an energetic, well-integrated crew of fifty-four men. His captain noted that "he uses all his abilities to further the interests of the service," that he had "every confidence in his sangfroid and discernment," and that de Prévaux was "well-suited for command."

A year later, Jacques was overjoyed to hear that his application to be transferred to the Naval Air Service had finally been accepted. Everything followed very quickly: three months' instruction at the Saint-Cyr training center for airship pilots, his certificate, his promotion, his nomination as commander of the Rinxent base. At last he was on course for the prestigious career that his Naval College superiors had predicted.

3

AIRSHIP PILOT

There was a thick fog on that October afternoon in 1917, and it was hard to make out the twists and turns in the road from Boulogne to Calais. Here and there, puddles of dirty water marked the potholes left by the shelling, whose muffled echoes could occasionally be heard. About fifteen kilometers from Boulogne, there was a bend in the road where it crossed the Slack, a muddy little river that came out on the beach at Ambleteuse, south of the cliffs of Cape Gris-Nez. The Marquise-Rinxent base was a little to the right, at the end of a path bristling with barbed wire. At the fork in the road the typical base hangars and hydrogen factory came into sight.

In a large front-wheel-drive car traveling in that direction was the new base commander, sitting in the back in full-dress uniform. He had come to take up his post and was going over the names of his predecessors; there had already been four since the creation of the base in January the previous year. What was the matter with Rinxent, that it had gone through so many commanders? Leaning back on the cushions with a nonchalance he didn't feel, his legs crossed as always (even in official photos) Jacques de Prévaux smoked cigarette after cigarette, feigning the indifferent air appropriate to his rank. At twenty-nine, he had mastered his almost pathological shyness, or rather he had transformed it into a reserve that attracted more respect than straightforward comradeship, and accentuated the air of nobility that emanated from him. Though not charming,—too weak a term for this austere man—he was strangely attractive: a big forehead, a stubborn jaw, which compensated for the sensuality of his mouth, a permanently intense gaze, and very beautiful hands. It was easy to imagine that he could be irresistible, if only he would smile.

The car passed through the barrier at the entrance to the base. De Prévaux, impassive, saluted, concealing the emotion that gripped him at this symbolic moment of his life in the navy: his first command, with which he had finally been entrusted, seven years after leaving the Naval College. For an instant his pride was mingled with a touch of anxiety. Would he be capable of commanding older men, seeing that his appointment was so recent and that he had had so little experience of marine aviation? But no sooner had they surfaced than his doubts disappeared. Nothing could undermine his joy at being given a command, or his relief at realizing that the grim years were over. Those ordeals, that lassitude, the fits of melancholy that had made him doubt both himself and his career, were now in the past. He had come alive again, he was saved. In two months everything had changed, so quickly that once again he took a childish pleasure in going over the proofs of it: his third stripe, making him a lieutenant commander, his brand-new airship pilot's badge (an anchor and two wings), the letter appointing him commander of the Marquise-Rinxent center, signed by the minister of the navy who "enjoined all the personnel of the service to recognize him as their commander, and to obey all his orders for the benefit of the service and the success of the French fighting forces." A formula that he knew by heart and he was sure he would often read again, and for more prestigious assignments. It was a new man, sure of his abilities, who was taking control of Rinxent, a man born to command.

The sailors were lined up on the modest parade ground in

front of the main building. The mist had just cleared, and the cool autumn sun was glistening on the metal structures, the masts, cables, telegraph wires, and the badges on the men's uniforms. The bugle announced the arrival of the commander, the men stood stiffly at attention, and Jacques straightened up to make himself look taller, a reflex that dated from his time at the Naval College, when he had regretted that he was of no more than average height and had been driven to despair by the daily ordeal of lining up on parade. At such times he resented the Trolley de Prévaux family for their small stature, which he had inherited and which, he thought, deprived him of the bearing indispensable to the exercise of authority. He made up for this defect by adopting a certain rigidity.

After a few speeches, a rather shrill "Marseillaise," and the review of his crews, de Prévaux took up his post as commander. He had about a hundred ordinary seamen and petty officers under his command, in addition to the airship captains. On his way to the mess, where there was to be a brief reception for the officers, de Prévaux once again thought that it would not be easy to impose his authority on the pilots. Their experience exceeded his—he had only had his certificate for three weeks, and his promotion for two months. What was more, he had skipped the normal stages of a military career—he should have started as a second officer and then become captain of an airship. The fact that he had been directly appointed head of an air base was thanks to his seniority in the navy, and also because naval aviation was expanding fast, and in urgent need of officers.

The Naval Air Service had been created in 1912—and was comprised of two aircraft. (French military aviation was only three years older.) It had had a difficult beginning; sailors weren't convinced that aircraft would be of any use, and military circles doubted the soundness of such fragile machines. "War isn't made with toys that are at the mercy of natural forces," wrote a specialist journal in 1910, greeting this new "fad," the airplane, with derision, and begging the minister "to put an end to this abominable joke." And anyway, the antics of the general staff had nearly sunk the project. One of their two aircraft, a seaplane, was based at the edge of a pond, which was almost always bone dry, while the other, a biplane, couldn't take off from its landing strip, which was often flooded. When war broke out, the French Naval Air Service was proud to count twenty-five planes and fourteen licensed pilots, while at the same time Great Britain had acquired about a hundred aircraft and ten dirigibles. Germany, for its part, had devoted its resources to gigantic bombing airships, the famous zeppelins.

The first months of hostilities had overcome this skepticism. On the one hand, the damage caused by German aerial bombardment proved how effective fighters and seaplanes could be. On the other, the need to detect and fight the enemy submarines drove the French to reinforce their air-surveillance patrols as a part of their naval combat forces. Airships were the ideal weapon—ships had not yet been equipped with antiaircraft guns. Silent, or practically so, invisible at night, easily able to adjust their altitude, capable of remaining motionless above their target, airships had a unique view of the depths, and no submarine could escape the vigilance of their crew. Equipped for bombing, they could also guide the ships' fire—sometimes simply by talking to the crew, since they were often within hailing distance and could remain static just a few meters above the surface of the water. Complementary to the aircraft of those days, they in some respects surpassed them, particularly in terms of the ability to stay aloft for extended periods. In 1919 the biggest airship beat by several hours the existing record for continuous flight of four days. They could travel 70 kilometers per hour at a time when airplanes could not fly faster than 100 kph. Their Achilles' heel was bad weather: heavy squalls and storms were responsible for the only losses of naval airships throughout the conflict.

In that period of the war, funds were released without argument, and the Naval Air Service developed rapidly. By the end of 1919, it had at its disposal 700 aircraft, with 460 pilots on the active list—a level it was never to regain—and also some twenty armed airships.

They were almost all prototypes, fine-tuned by eccentric engineers who, in freezing hangars open to the north wind, fiddled about with fantastic systems of various kinds of valves concocted to give the thing more stability or make it easier to maneuver. They would concoct a chancy prototype and extract permission from the commander to try it in the air. The first flight of any craft was always an adventure.

The day after he arrived, de Prévaux watched the departure on patrol, over the southwestern zone of the Pas de Calais, of one of the four airships based in Marquise-Rinxent. These were *vedettes* (scouts), 48 meters long. They had two 80-horsepower engines, which were used only for propulsion, as an airship gains altitude by releasing ballast and descends by letting out gas. In the vast wooden hangar, the airship would be dozing, half inflated. Just a little more hydrogen and the rubberized envelope would start to shudder, and then stretch, with a noise like paper being smoothed out. As its volume of 2,800 cubic meters began to fill, the VZ (V for *Vedette,* Z for *Zodiac,* its manufacturer) would once again take on the cigar shape that distinguishes airships from balloons. Standing to attention on either side, the ground crew await orders. The men bring the *vedette* out of the hangar and its loading area, tow it over the airfield and immobilize it, head to wind, while the crew—pilot, radio operator and mechanic—get into the flimsy gondola suspended from the hull. The engine and trim are tested. All in order—the *vedette* can take off. At the rudder, the sublieutenant finally gives the command "Let go!"—the order to empty the water bags that constitute the ballast—and while the dripping-wet men shake themselves and grumble, the airship gently rises straight up into the clear sky.

The *vedette*'s mission is to spot enemy mines and submarines. This is routine for all the VZs at the Marquise-Rinxent air base. Patrolling for several hours on end, their heads outside the gondola, their eyes wide open and fixed on the sea, the crew search for the distinctive outline of a submerged submarine. Most of the time all they can see is a vague shadow moving through the opaque depths, or a suspicious-looking wake. The mines scattered around the entry to the ports are easier to make out, but discovering them is less exciting for the crew, who have to content themselves with signaling their position to the surface craft, whose job it is to blow them up. On a day with excellent visibility the crew of the *vedette* concentrate even harder—they want to show the new commander how efficient they are—and the VZ finally spots a submarine. Activating stations on board, they release the two 50-kilogram bombs carried under the gondola. The three men peer through the muddy wash for the trail of diesel oil that will show they've scored a bull's-eye, that at least one enemy craft has been damaged. Yes, they have hit it; they drop a little buoy to mark the spot and, before returning to base, they call up a British seaplane patrolling nearby and ask for reinforcements. The commander will be pleased.

The sailors had taken to airships from the beginning. They found they had a curious affinity with lighter-than-air craft, no doubt because, unlike airplanes, balloons and airships hover on a level with the waves and their crews work in the open air—and both air and water are the natural elements of the navigator. Besides, an airship doesn't take off, but "takes to the air as a boat to the sea," and the terminology employed is generally naval. Captain de Brossard, the last naval airship captain, explained this attraction: "I was happy on my torpedo boat. . . . I liked it, I did indeed. Still, I felt I wanted something more. I suddenly wanted to see the sea as a whole, from a more elevated viewpoint than the crest of the waves: the sea and its ships, their wakes, and the ballets the squadrons traced on the waves, like diagrams. Then I would have the impression that they all belonged to me. . . . I knew that an essential part of the game was going to be played out in the sea clouds. A real seaman's game. I didn't want to miss that."

It took only a few months for de Prévaux to feel at home in Marquise-Rinxent. There was no shortage of work. Each day he organized the turnaround of the patrol flights, the meticulous inspection of the airships, the review of the crews, and wrote the reports. In peacetime, this would have been no problem. But under the enemy bombing raids, the slightest sortie became dangerous, and the missions followed one another without a break. He got used to it. When he had been on the *Chasseur* three years previously, off the Greek coast, he had anxiously wondered how he would stand up under fire. Now he was reassured that he wouldn't flinch. And in any case, he had been awarded the croix de guerre and the Legion of Honor. He was no more than irritated if some problem obliged him to cancel one of his various rendezvous. The passionate young man had given way to an officer who was sure of himself. The center was flourishing, and its commander was acquitting himself well. He had broken himself of his opium habit and had once again begun to make notes of what he read. He had organized a peaceful social life for himself, based on dinners with lieutenant commanders and their wives, visits to the theater in Boulogne, tea parties with a few society ladies, and pleasant evenings with Lucette or Andrée. A full, well-regulated life.

All he lacked, at the core of his life and being, was a great love.

4

RANK AND RESPECTABILITY

B landine Ollivier was to be the lucky lady. Jacques met her
in Paris in June 1919; they wrote to each other and went to
concerts and the Bois de Boulogne together. Since it was not
done to go out with an upper-class young lady without having
been approved by her parents, Jacques was introduced, and
subjected himself to their scrutiny. He had no trouble in making
himself agreeable, and captivated them. He was given permission to pay his addresses to Blandine.

This time it was serious. He was caught. He had to speak to
his father as soon as possible. In the car taking him to Lille, he
tried to work out how to paint Blandine in a favorable light,
because he suspected that his father would disapprove of his
choice. Not that this marriage would be a misalliance. The
haute bourgeois Olliviers held a considerable position in society. Blandine's grandfather, Emile Ollivier, had been a minister under Napoleon III, the very man who had boasted that he
had had the 1870 war voted through "with a light heart." He
had married another Blandine, one of the two daughters of
Liszt and the Countess Marie d'Agoult, the other daughter
being Cosima Wagner. So even though Jacques' future fiancée
had serious musical connections and society references, in the
eyes of the very austere Alfred Trolley de Prévaux, this was
more like a handicap. But his youngest son's radiant, deter-

mined air overcame his criticisms, and Jacques left Lille reassured.

Now that he was firmly established in his military career, all he needed to make him feel completely respectable was a wife. He was beginning to tire of flirtations with girls glimpsed at the theater, as he was of his facile liaisons with Lucette and Andrée, the two young women in Boulogne whom he took to the casino by turns.

By the grace of God, the maternal branch of the Trolley de Prévaux family had numerous connections in society and he had asked various well-placed aunts to find him a suitable girl. Rinxent was not far from Paris, and consequently he spent all his leave in the capital. No sooner had he left his suitcase at the Military Club than he rushed off to the barber's, the tailor's, the glovemaker's, because he wanted the dice loaded in his favor. He became frivolous, but methodically so. Aunt Antonine gave a tea party, Aunt Prisse got him invited to an elegant *vernissage,* Aunt Auffray planned a lunch that would certainly be decisive for him. In vain. There was no shortage of possible candidates, but he always found some fault with them. Back at the base, he spoke of his disappointment at the stupidity of society women, however pretty and elegant: "But can one just look at them without saying anything?" All in all, he preferred the affection that Lucette and little Andrée so willingly gave him. No doubt he was demanding too much—both beauty and intelligence, and love as a bonus. At thirty-one he was still an incurable romantic.

Roland mocked his cousin, deploring the fact that he was aspiring to a future of slippers embroidered by a virtuous spouse. He sincerely pitied Jacques for wasting his leave interviewing hordes of innocent young girls.

Yet it was the cynical Roland who introduced Jacques to Blandine. She was a great friend of Jenny Fabre-Luce, a young woman who was having a passionate and much-disapproved-of affair with Roland (they married not long afterwards). What can it have been in Blandine that appealed to Jacques? People thought she had admirable eyes and hair, and (said Roland) she had "an unusual face, a rare quality, preferable to banal beauty." She had a lot of personality; she was cultured and, of course, a remarkable musician. For Blandine it was love at first sight. She took the initiative and threw herself at the naval officer with beautiful eyes who always looked so solemn. Jacques asked nothing better than to fall in love, and Blandine bore no resemblance to the innocent young girls Roland thought so ridiculous. Suddenly he felt only pity for Lucette and Andrée, and added the correspondence of Liszt and Wagner to his current reading of Spinoza and an account of the Battle of Jutland.

The Olliviers owned a vast estate in Sainte-Maxime. Jacques was invited there three months after he had met their daughter. It was a crucial visit. He trembled as he prepared himself for it. There would be man-to-man conversations with Daniel Ollivier, confidential talks with Blandine's mother, and, if all went well, a few private moments with the girl, in the grounds, which he imagined thickly wooded. On the third evening, he solemnly asked her parents for her hand. Catherine Ollivier had been won over by Jacques' charm, and her consent had been given from the start. They had had long conversations about religion, and the mother congratulated herself on seeing her frivolous daughter becoming a member of a practicing Catholic family. The father's agreement was more difficult to obtain: de Prévaux had had to confess his slender means. But his wife's praise and his daughter's obvious happiness finally overcame his doubts. The marriage would take place with great ceremony in the fashionable parish of Saint-Augustin in April 1920. Jacques was overcome with joy.

And yet he was bored. With the war over, his interest in commanding Marquise-Rinxent diminished considerably. Besides, even the continuing existence of the base was in doubt. After 1918, military budgets were sharply reduced, and an inquiry was launched into probable future needs, the upshot of which was that available resources were to be redistributed so that only a few centers of naval aviation would benefit. The decision to close down Rinxent was made in the summer of 1919, and de Prévaux became anxious about his next posting. He was pretty sure of the promotion to which he was entitled by his good reports and his mentions in dispatches, but simply sitting and waiting, he risked being forgotten. He worked to give the decision a helping hand. Traveling back and forth between Boulogne and Paris, Jacques laid siege to friends in the ministry and bombarded Roland with urgent letters. Roland's father, Pierre de Margerie, had just been made ambassador to Belgium, and the post of naval attaché in Brussels would be tempting. But no such post was to be created. Logically enough, the Treaty of Versailles forbade a disarmed Germany to nominate military attachés; therefore, in the name of reciprocity, the Allies could not have any either. It wasn't until 1926 that these posts were restored.

Finally, in the autumn, de Prévaux was told that he was to leave Marquise-Rinxent, but only to take command of another airship center: in Montebourg, on the Cotentin peninsula in Normandy. The base was actually in the village of Ecausseville and was one of the four remaining home ports for airships, as well as for English Sea Scouts, whose volume was no more than 1,800 cubic meters. This was not a promotion, particularly as Montebourg was also scheluled to be closed. Jacques took up his post in November and for three months led a monastic life full of boring tasks: getting the airships disarmed, their envelopes folded, their gondolas dismantled, and sending the whole lot to Rochefort, writing the inevitable reports. He continued his efforts to get another posting—for it was unthinkable that he should bring Blandine to such an out-of-the-way place as Montebourg—and also to find a replacement who would agree to take over from him. For their part, the Olliviers in Paris exercised their influence to get their future son-in-law appointed to a worthy post.

Eventually, one of de Prévaux's friends sounded him out about a possible appointment to the departmental staff of the ministry of the navy. He was flattered, but hesitated. Naturally, Blandine and her parents would be delighted for the young couple to settle in Paris, but should he give up hope of another command? Perhaps even of a seagoing command? Or of a diplomatic post? How should he decide between what was reasonable and what he really wanted, deep down? Useless questions. He knew very well that the job he was being offered was one he couldn't refuse. In February, de Prévaux was appointed to the personal staff of the navy minister (Adolphe Landry, and later Gabriel Guist'hau).

His new colleagues welcomed him coolly. His nomination was so obviously due to the good offices of the minister that they took it for granted he wouldn't be up to the job. Jacques accepted the challenge and worked hard to acquire the necessary skills. He found his liking for methodical work extremely useful, and by studying the reports on military strategy he soon became familiar with diplomatic questions. His superiors lavished praise on this captain, who seemed to be made for posts on the General Staff or to be a representative of his country abroad. The minister's principal private secretary recommended him as "a first-class officer, such as we rarely encounter," and said that it would be in the interests of the navy to see that he was advanced rapidly.

De Prévaux remained on the minister's departmental staff for two years. In January 1922 he was appointed commander of the minesweeping flotilla of the Toulon fifth district and to the personal command of the gunboat *Diligente*. But he was in poor health and had to take two months' convalescent leave for debility and chronic fatigue. Finally, on June 1, 1924, he was made commander of naval aviation in Cuers-Pierrefeu, in the Var near Toulon. In the meantime, he had been promoted to lieutenant commander.

Once again, de Prévaux entered a naval aviation base with much pomp and ceremony. As he saluted the sailors lined up in the hot sun, he thought what a long way he had come since that day in 1917 when he had arrived at Marquise-Rinxent full of apprehension and excitement. Not that he denied the elation of the moment; it was a natural stage in the career of an officer. He was amused to remember the feelings that had overwhelmed him, and above all the bizarre impression of coming back to life. From what? What had happened to him that was so terrible? Every time Jacques tried to think back to the years preceding his first command, he seemed to be surrounded by a vague fog, as if he had decided to forget them. On the other hand, he remembered perfectly that at Rinxent he had drawn a line under his youth. He could still see himself sitting at his desk covered with books and dossiers—he hadn't yet become methodical—writing in his diary. It was nighttime, or at least late evening. He could hear the wind whistling in the shrouds; he had just started on a new packet of cigarettes.

"The education I was given," he wrote, "was designed to make me as banal as everyone else, to fit me to live in an artificial moral setting. . . . People like me, who one day discover that there is something else and cannot live according to formulas, dogmas or books, have to waste ten years in tearing off the mask of banality, in rediscovering themselves and finding a role attuned to real life. . . . And then it is too late to give all they can." Jacques straightened up proudly. No, for him, it was not too late.

* * *

At Cuers, Jacques discovered another type of dirigible, the rigid airships. The *vedettes* he had piloted at Rinxent had a directly inflatable envelope, but these giant vessels had a rigid metal framework enclosing ballonets inflated with hydrogen or helium. The Cuers base was opened in 1919 to house the big rigid airships, which the General Staff, fascinated by the success of the German zeppelins during the war, was determined to acquire. These flying monsters needed made-to-measure airports and, in particular, hangars 250 meters long and 45 meters high, hydrogen factories—there were two at Cuers—and a gasometer with a capacity of 10,000 cubic meters. All these installations, added to those needed for the smaller *vedettes* and escort craft, made Cuers the largest air base in France. However, wedged between steep mountains and the sea, and subject to the ravages of the mistral, the site was badly chosen, and the pilots frequently had to perform tricky maneuvers.

The first big rigid airship had arrived in 1920—too early, as the hangars had not been completed. It had had to be deflated. This colossus, 226 meters long, was one of the two zeppelins the Germans had been forced to surrender to France by way of reparations. It was rechristened the *Dixmude,* after a town in Belgium heroically defended by French marines. Its commander, Lieutenant Commander Jean du Plessis de Grenedan, had taken delivery of it at Maubeuge and, with a thirty-nine-man crew, had managed to get it to Cuers. This was already something of an exploit, since the Germans had handed it over to France in a lamentable condition and "forgotten" to include its technical documents. When the hangar was at last finished and they tried to reinflate the zeppelin, they found that the ballonets showed signs of age and had become porous. They deflated it again, but it took du Plessis several more years to get the green light from the navy department for the funds to manufacture new ballonets. And so it was not until August 1923 that the 68,500 cubic meters of the *Dixmude* were again inflated and it could take to the air. The six trips made by the giant cigar were all successful; it even beat the world nonstop flight record (118 hours and 9,000 kilometers). The seventh sortie ended tragically. Caught in a storm, the *Dixmude* was struck by lightning over Sicily on December 21, 1923, and crashed, killing all on board. De Prévaux arrived in Cuers six months later.

He was to pilot the second zeppelin, the former *Nordstern*, rechristened *Méditerranée*. Landing after a twelve-hour sortie, he had the impression of descending from a cloud. In spite of its smaller size, only 130 meters long, the zeppelin had amazing stability. It glided noiselessly, effortlessly, as if it was in its element, and it was unaffected by air pockets. In the warmth of the cabin, dimly lit by a few lamps, it was so comfortable that it was possible to write. The catastrophe of the *Dixmude* nearly caused the *Méditerranée* to be grounded. When de Prévaux took command at Cuers, the captain of the zeppelin put up a fight to get permission from the General Staff to attempt at least one more sortie. Jacques supported him, the *Méditerranée* was reprieved, and service was resumed. The end of the rigid airships came when the *Méditerranée* was scrapped in September 1926, and this was the beginning of the end of lighter-than-air craft.

Cuers not only housed these two airships, the dirigible study group based there was engaged in all sorts of experiments. It was also the base for a bomber squadron which, with its six 5-tonne Goliath planes that could be equipped with either wheels or pontoons, was later to join the Spanish Air Force in the war of the Rif.

For two years, de Prévaux was in command of a center that pursued varied activities, and at a turning point in the development of aeronautics. He was still very highly regarded by his superiors: "He is an absolutely first-rate officer who must be given command as often as possible and be rapidly promoted," wrote the commander of naval aviation on the Mediterranean coasts.

* * *

Promotion—de Prévaux wanted nothing better. True, he was passionately interested in his Cuers command and led a pleasant life in the Midi with Blandine and their two daughters. However, the way plans for the future use of lighter-than-air craft were developing troubled him; he foresaw that they would inevitably be made obsolete and replaced by airplanes. Moreover, he had not given up the idea of going into the diplomatic service. His stint on the minister's staff and his command of the southern zone had given him a taste for strategy and diplomacy. For the last ten years or so, his superiors had been noting in his record book that he would make a very good naval attaché. It was time to find out whether he was indeed qualified for such a post. In the autumn of 1925 there was talk of appointing a naval attaché to Rome. This would be a splendid post; as an art lover, de Prévaux found it very tempting, and Blandine, who spoke Italian, would have been ideally suited to it. But although he called on all his influential friends in high places and had the support of the General Staff and the ambassador to Rome, who asked for him by name, the minister of the navy, Emile Borel, chose his rival. De Prévaux had to wait another year until Georges Leygues, once again a minister, finally made him a naval attaché.

He was posted to Berlin.

5
NAVAL ATTACHÉ IN BERLIN

September 1930. Dusk was falling softly over Berlin and, on the warm night air, distant noises from the streets were coming through the open casement window—laughter, cars passing over cobblestones, streetcars rattling—sounds muffled only by the willows lining the Bendlerstrasse. Standing at the window in his shirtsleeves, smoking, Jacques was absently watching the street lamps gradually light up through the foliage. After four years of Berlin life, this picturesque scene no longer affected him. It was life at sea that stirred him—immaculate ships, night watches on the bridge, sailors standing at attention to salute the colors in the freezing early hours, the atmosphere of military camaraderie—these, rather than fashionable soirées, were what would make him completely happy.

Was he never going to be satisfied then? At forty-two he was still trying to find himself, he thought despondently. He had fought to get this naval attaché job, a terrific job, and he had made a success of it, but now all he dreamed of was going back to sea. He might as well be honest with himself: he had been delighted to immerse himself in a life of diplomacy, of pretense, all superficiality and ease. It had done wonders for his self-esteem and he had enjoyed it. Nevertheless, he had a vague impression that he was losing himself. He had been more demanding when he was young. His love life was another disappointment. He and Blandine no longer had anything in common. As for the young women who so agreeably occupied his nights, they didn't count. It made him smile, though, when he thought of them, and it brought him back to the present. Introspection is unhealthy, the Jesuits of his childhood would have said. He shrugged his shoulders and turned his mind back to that night's reception.

Shutting the jade box from which he had taken cuff links emblazoned with his coat of arms, he put them on. His orderly helped him on with his newly pressed dinner jacket, then, at a sign from him, withdrew. Jacques absentmindedly took a cigarette, rolled it around in his nicotine-stained fingers, and lit it as he crossed the room. The reflection he studied in the big mirror of the paneled bedroom satisfied him. It showed the solid figure of a mature man who wore his clothes with the ease of one used to uniforms. He was a little stocky, maybe, but the intensity of his clear gaze, the impression of strength made by his broad shoulders and stubborn chin, his whole bearing, had given him a charisma that struck everyone who met him. He was now well aware of his power of seduction and of the spell he cast over the men under his orders. His service record contained this curt appraisal: "He knows his worth." He already had a glittering career behind him, and anyway, he had been promoted to commander in 1928, and so far he had acquitted himself admirably in Berlin.

It was a difficult mission. De Prévaux was the first naval attaché since the war. He had arrived on October 15, 1926, to find himself in an environment hostile to everything French and military. The Locarno Pact had not been signed until the previous year, and the Ruhr had only just been evacuated. There was still bitter resentment, and the chief of naval staff, Admiral Salaun, recognized that the mission of the naval attaché was extremely delicate and required an abundance of diplomatic finesse.

The Germany Jacques discovered had in theory been disarmed. The imperial Reich had been ordered by the Treaty of Versailles to reduce its armed forces and destroy most of its weapons. After innumerable difficulties, they had reached the final stages of the disarmament process. The deliberations of the Interallied Military Control Commission came to an end only in 1927, after years of contending with the ill will, and bad faith, of the defeated. In this context, the mandate of the military attachés was even more absurd: they had to report on military aviation, whereas the Treaty of Versailles had forbidden Germany to have any such thing. And yet there was indeed vital information to be gathered. For while Germany was officially disarmed, she was secretly rearming; what was more, she was modernizing her forces. Even before the commission experts charged to oversee the disarmament process had packed their bags, the Reichswehr, discreetly and outside its frontiers, was perfecting prototypes of the modern weapons that were to replace the obsolete equipment painfully confiscated by the Allies. Thus, in Vigo, Kronstadt and Sebastopol, German engineers were supervising the assembly of ultramodern submarines, which largely compensated for the 315 submarines destroyed by the commission, and preparing a high-performance navy. These designs were top secret, yet the naval attaché must have observed that the Reich, even disarmed and temporarily powerless, had lost little of its strength.

The French ambassador, Pierre de Margerie, had warmly welcomed the new naval attaché and had opened the doors of fashionable Berlin. Jacques' maternal uncle, de Margerie was at the zenith of his career. Stationed in Berlin since 1922, this refined, cultured man of the world, well known for his feminine conquests, had made his palace in the Pariser Platz into a crossroads of elegant and artistic Berlin. Memories of sumptuous receptions he gave there remained with his guests long afterwards: the bewigged lackeys stationed on each step of the monumental staircase sweeping up on both sides, the richly laden tables and the flowers that adorned them, formed a magnificent setting for formal banquets.

His first secretary was his son Roland, Jacques' cousin, the one who signed his letters "your old brother," and whose friendship was to be unfailing. When Jacques, ten years later, decided to get a divorce and remarry, Roland was the only one in the whole family to give him his moral—and financial—support. It was Roland and his wife, Jenny, who had advised Jacques to apply for the post of naval attaché in Berlin. They had reassured the couple about the conditions of life in the German capital, which had greatly improved since they themselves had arrived in 1923. Life was expensive, true, but stable and pleasant. There were all sorts of things in the shops, and above all, the French were finally able to meet Berliners without risking unpleasant incidents, which were still very frequent at the beginning of the twenties. Blandine was delighted to be reunited with Jenny, who was their elder daughter's godmother.

The two cousins resumed their friendship. They had the same interests: both were prodigious readers, their appetites never satisfied. Both were passionately interested in the new cultural trends then absorbing the German intelligentsia, and together they explored the exciting life of the capital. Roland, who always kept the six or seven volumes of the Almanach de Gotha at hand, gave his older cousin the benefit of his intimate knowledge of Berlin society.

Jacques was fascinated by the abundance of Berlin's cultural life. His previous posts, in the provinces or at sea, had not accustomed him to such creative audacity. At the end of the twenties, Berlin was buzzing with intense artistic activity. The return of prosperity, thanks to the American credits which propped up the German economy until the Wall Street crash of October 1929, had given Berliners a craving for entertainment and had created new art forms. This golden age, which was soon to end abruptly when the Nazis came to power, saw the success of Bertolt Brecht and the scandal caused by his *Threepenny Opera* at its premiere on August 31, 1928. The cinema was commanding attention as an indisputable art form—*The Blue Angel* dates from 1930—and Marlene Dietrich was a tremendous success in the Tingel Tangel cabaret in the Kantstrasse. Yehudi Menuhin gave one of his first recitals to a thrilled audience. The best American jazz orchestras were enthusiastically received.

The French embassy played its part in this effervescence; it received the French artists who had been drawn to Berlin and became the center of cultural exchanges. When, on January 16, 1928, André Gide, accompanied by Marc Allégret and other friends, came to give a lecture, he stayed with the Viénots, who were friends of Roland and Jacques. At the same time the surrealist writer René Crevel, who was twenty-eight and had just published *A Difficult Death,* was living in Berlin, where he divided his time between homosexual cabarets and Dorothea Sternheim, who was nicknamed Mopse or Mopsa. Still very young at that time, she was a familiar figure in artistic Berlin. The daughter of the playwright Carl Sternheim, a friend of the Mann family, in particular of Klaus, (she designed the sets for his plays), she was a member of the extravagant circles that revolutionized artistic conventions. Even in Berlin, Mopse shocked people with her short hair and her boy's clothes, loving both men and women. Photos from this period show her as a sturdy girl with a radiant smile, and beautiful in an aggressively provocative way. Was it her robust health that attracted Crevel, who was already suffering from tuberculosis? In any case, they met in Berlin and were virtually inseparable. When Gide arrived in the capital, the two groups merged. And it was at de Prévaux's flat that a large dinner was organized in honor of René Crevel, after a lecture he gave at the university in the presence of everyone who was anyone in literary Berlin and, of course, Mopse.

The city expressed its relief that the grim postwar years had finally come to an end by lightheartedly indulging in the frenzied pursuit of pleasure. From Unter den Linden to the Potsdamer Platz, the center of Berlin flaunted the unprecedented luxury of its legendary hotels, its elegant cafés and fashionable boutiques. Its nightlife, not to be outdone, boasted its nightclubs, some reserved for transvestites, its revues, its cabarets, its unbridled private soirées, its orgies. Salons were transformed into dance halls. Party followed party, each vying with the others to be the gayest. Berlin was the capital of pleasure. Jacques was soon caught up in this whirlwind. His previous posts had deprived this rather severe man of such distractions. Now he threw himself wholeheartedly into the prevailing spirit of frivolity. Moreover, it was in Berlin that he got into his nocturnal habits, which were to become notorious in the navy and would remain associated with his name.

But de Prévaux didn't restrict himself to appearing at balls and literary salons. During a dinner in the Pariser Platz, he had met Pierre Viénot, and through him became interested in the efforts of the Franco-German Committee for Information and Documentation, which Viénot had set up in 1926. Viénot was convinced that a prosperous and peaceful Germany could play a positive role within Europe, that a new conflict must be avoided at all costs, and that it was an absolute priority for France and Germany to be reconciled. Their governments, blinded by nationalistic sentiments, were incapable of going beyond ideas of revenge. So the business of reconciliation would have to come from a different quarter, and start by informing and detoxifying public opinion.

Viénot had submitted his plan to the French embassy: the committee would be based in Paris and Berlin and composed of intellectuals, industrialists and financiers—the only people, Viénot thought, capable of not thinking in nationalistic terms.

Naturally, they would all be of unimpeachable character, the elite of the two countries. For several months the de Margeries, father and son, were to take part in discussions on the composition of the French side of the committee. Both the French and German groups would finally have thirty-five members, among whom would be the Duc de Broglie, Wladimir d'Ormesson, André Siegfried, the presidents of Krupp and Thyssen, and some bankers. Viénot himself was the Berlin "delegate" of the French group, which met for the first time in November 1926. For president of the committee he had proposed Emile Mayrisch, an influential industrialist from Luxembourg, who had founded and for a long time presided over one of the principal European metallurgical conglomerates, the Arbed. Every writer and book lover in Europe flocked to the salons of his wife, née Aline de Saint-Hubert, in their Colpach castle. Shortly afterwards, Pierre Viénot married their daughter Andrée.

Immediately after his arrival in Berlin, de Prévaux immersed himself in this Franco-German adventure, which was to leave its indelible mark on everyone involved. The committee meetings took place in the impassioned atmosphere of a shared ideal of fraternity, to which no small contribution was made by the lavish dinners the embassy provided. Viénot, who was very much at home in the Pariser Platz, brought all the most interesting and influential personalities there with him. He was the unofficial intermediary between France and Germany, and he made the committee into a pressure group lobbying for peace.

But set against increasing difficulties, the committee's task was gradually made impossible. The political climate was poisoned by the failure of the disarmament conference, by the polemics and violent reactions of German public opinion to the Young plan for the settlement of reparations. Despite all the efforts made by Viénot and Pierre de Margerie to clear up what they liked to think of as misunderstandings, mutual confidence slowly evaporated. The committee was dissolved in 1933. In the meantime, Viénot had left Germany (in December 1929), de Prévaux a year later, then Pierre de Margerie, and finally Roland. By then the National Socialists had seized power.

At the end of the twenties, neither Viénot nor Ambassador de Margerie had been aware of the seriousness of the danger threatening German democracy. Although they had witnessed the rise of Nazism, they underestimated its strength. But how could anyone at that time have conceived the possibility of the unthinkable actually happening?

They anxiously observed the growing misery of the people, galloping unemployment, the riots, like that of May 1, 1929, which left some thirty dead, the appeals to mobilization launched by the Communist Party, the barricades in the working-class district of Wedding, the marches which, in the red suburbs of Moabit and Neukölln, brought masses of demonstrating workers streaming through the center of Berlin. They could not be unaware of the nationalist propaganda of the Nazis, the demagogic articles in the press in the pay of Goebbels, the calls for revenge. They watched the impressive military parades and saw the enthusiasm they aroused in the crowds assembled along their routes. They noted the brand-new, high-performance equipment of the units, the exorbitant military budgets, the discipline of the soldiers. They were alarmed by the renewed outbreak of confrontations and violence. But could they have imagined that this would lead to Nazi totalitarianism? Admittedly, there were organizations of young fanatics, the storm troopers, the militia, and Adolf Hitler's talents as an orator and organizer—but recently he had not been flaunting the extremist ideas he had previously professed in the Munich beer halls. And besides, the electorate was showing itself to be reasonable, and remained faithful to the traditional political parties: the parties of the left had won a very big majority in the 1928 elections. In September 1930, though, the National Socialist Party won more than six million votes, and from twelve, the number of its members in the Reichstag went up to a hundred and seven, all of whom attended parliament in uniform. But the Socialist Party was still in the majority, and Brüning was still running the government. The situation in Germany was worrisome, particularly from the economic and social point of view, but not catastrophic.

When de Prévaux left Berlin at the end of 1930, he carried with him the image of a great nation, whose intellectual and economic leaders wanted peace. He was convinced that the Weimar Republic would be able to maintain political stability. He continued to champion reconciliation between the two peoples. His four years in Berlin left him a profound Germanophile.

The diplomatic corps and the elegant Berlin intellectual elite regretted de Prévaux's departure and deplored the stupid incident that had marred the last months of his term in office. Vermunt, a Dutch industrialist, had suspected his pretty young wife of being Jacques' mistress. He took it into his head to spy on his rival, followed him into a tearoom, lay in wait for him and slapped his face. A banal story of a deceived and comically violent husband, and in any case a strictly private affair. Nevertheless, it was maliciously exploited by the sensational press. On December 12, 1930, *Das kleine Journal,* which every week regaled its Berlin readers with the latest society gossip, announced fashionable balls, births of babies to people of consequence, and reported on elegant soirees, chose to splash the story of the altercation between de Prévaux and the jealous husband across four front-page columns with a banner headline. Their aim of creating a scandal and adding fuel to the anti-French campaigns was so obvious that Western diplomats stationed in Berlin knew it was a put-up job aimed at discrediting the diplomacy of a country belonging to the Entente. They closed ranks around de Prévaux, whose dignity they admired.

Blandine remained serene and haughtily declared that she had every confidence in her husband. Above all, appearances must be kept up, for the couple had long been estranged and they each went their own way. Jacques led an extensive and complicated love life, not through libertinage but from the need to exercise his powers of seduction. Nothing remained between him and Blandine other than a tacit agreement to put on an occasional show of living together as a couple. The children were no problem. The two little girls were entrusted to the care either of their governess or of their Ollivier grandparents.

When Jacques and Blandine returned to Paris in January 1931, the Olliviers refused to receive their son-in-law. In their judgment the "Berlin scandal" was intolerable, for a very precise reason: the rules of duels with pistols had not been respected. There had not even been a duel at all. Being ostracized by his wife's family left Jacques unmoved. The "scandal" hadn't bothered him; his closest friends, and in particular Roland de Margerie, hadn't stopped respecting him.

On his way to the ministry, where he was to be told of his next posting, Jacques felt strangely jubilant. The straitjacket he had been wearing in Berlin had finally burst at the seams. He was free, and available for the work he still had to accomplish.

6

ON THE CHINA SEAS

O n May 8, 1931, Jacques embarked for Shanghai, where he was to join the sloop *Altaïr,* of which he had just been given command. A month later he was climbing up the gangway while a deckhand piped him onboard in the manner appropriate to his rank. The *Altaïr* was a splendid ship, eighty-one meters from stem to stern and armed with four guns. She could reach seventeen knots, and was in fine trim. "Her two slender masts, her catwalks breaking the monotony of the hull, her harmonious overall lines, gave her an indisputable air of elegance. Her two 138-pounders added a military note, while the tricolor flag, still basking in the prestige of the 1918 victory, gave her the supreme attribute which carries so much weight in the Far East: face." The crew was composed of about a hundred men.

In the wardroom, de Prévaux got to know his staff. Apart from a marine engineer, a paymaster and a doctor, there were four young sublieutenants just out of the naval college. With them, as with his second-in-command, Lieutenant-Commander Robillard, there was the spontaneous atmosphere of respectful camaraderie that exists only at sea. These young officers shared his delight in being at sea and discovering new countries; they made a good team, full of enthusiasm for their work and full of vitality after it.

At nightfall Jacques leaned over the bulwarks and looked at

the harbor lights. Here at last at his feet lay China, the country he had been fascinated by since Jean Roulier had first told him about it twenty years before.... He could make out Shanghai's main thoroughfares, having studied its street map during the voyage. That brilliantly lit line along the Hwang-Poo was the Bund, some parts of it all aglow—cinemas, the flashing neon lights of the nightclubs—others were dark masses that had to be the foliage between the tall buildings of the insurance companies. Beyond, he could make out the district of the foreign concessions, with the lights of the villas glimmering here and there. Near the port, the Chinese town was darker, with vague patches of dim light; in the foreground, a few yellow navigation lights were reflected in the slimy black water of the roads. The *Altaïr* was anchored near enough to land for him to hear a hubbub carried over the water: a cacophony of new sounds, bizarre music, strangely modulated cries, all mixed with echoes of jazz and the familiar din of car horns.

What better introduction to China could there be than Shanghai, a populous, dissipated city whose insolent wealth, acquired from opium, was displayed along the Bund in apartment buildings and luxury hotels, a town of business and pleasure? Despite the humid heat and the occasional waft of decay, he suddenly wanted to be in the town, merging into the unknown, cosmopolitan crowd, rubbing shoulders with the swarming mass of coolies, strolling among those mysterious little shops, which he imagined contained treasure of jade, magic powders, opium pipes and enigmatic old Chinese men ...

His reverie was interrupted by a sailor who told him that the launch was ready to take him ashore. The captain of the *Altaïr* had been invited to the legation. Every evening he was to be invited either to Shanghai itself or to the *Primauguet,* the flagship of the commander in chief of the naval forces in the Far East, when he wasn't receiving aboard his own ship authorities and notables, merchants and representatives of the chamber of commerce, consuls and officers from other ships. The work of a diplomat, in short, for which he was perfectly qualified.

De Prévaux came to life again. He was proud and happy to have a seagoing command at last, and moreover in China, which every sailor dreams of. And besides, as Vice Admiral Berthelot was absent, he was lucky enough to replace him as senior officer of the French ships in the Shanghai roads. Under his orders, the *Altaïr* was to crisscross the China seas from Japan to the Philippines, going the rounds of the concessions and French territories in the Far East. During his first six months the sloop patrolled between Shanghai, Nanking and Hankow (now part of Wuhan), sailing up the Yangtze River. Then she headed for Japan, called at Nagasaki, and paid a long visit to the Miyajima sanctuary in the bay of Hiroshima before casting anchor at Kobe. Next there were six more months on patrol around Shanghai, then the long crossing of the East China Sea down to the South China Sea, putting in at Amoy (now Xiamen), Keelung, Taiwan's big port, Hong Kong, Fort Bayard (now Zhanjiang), a territory leased to France, the Bay of Along, and finally Manila. Each port call, with the sloop proudly flying the national flag, became an occasion to reaffirm France's possession of these parcels of oriental land.

These enjoyable voyages gave him a chance to meet and have fascinating conversations with cultivated Sinophile Europeans. Jacques decided to make a serious study of Chinese. He found a teacher in Shanghai who had no objection to teaching a French officer and was willing to fit in with his irregular schedules. He was an old Chinese scholar who had been a tutor to aristocratic families before the advent of the republic, and who still enjoyed a reputation as a great authority on Mandarin. Each time he entered his house, Jacques was fascinated by his teacher's collection of old ivories. Old Chang took a liking to his diligent student, and as a good-bye present gave him an ivory statuette Jacques had fallen in love with, which he called

"The Chinese Virgin" because of her arching hips and the folds of her dress, which followed the curves of the elephant's tusk. And together with the language, Chang taught him a few rudiments of the wisdom of the East, and some subtleties in the use of opium.

Jacques threw himself wholeheartedly into the study of Buddhism. He had always been very religious. When he was quite small, his parents had given him a "game of mass," which he enjoyed playing with, piously handling the doll's chasuble and the minute ciboria. The only serious disagreement he had had with Blandine wàs of a religious nature. She had been brought up in the Ollivier tradition of free thought and had at first refused to take communion at their wedding mass; it had needed all Jacques' strength of conviction, with the complicity of the very Catholic Catherine Ollivier, to get her to see reason. In Shanghai and Saigon, Jacques got a list of works on Buddhism available in the libraries. He read everything he could find on the subject and took notes, which gradually became commentaries. He discovered The Tibetan Book of the Dead and was dazzled by it. Becoming familiar in this way with other forms of religious thought, even if, strictly speaking, it was more a question of ethics than of religion, he built up his own spiritual syncretism. His Catholicism became purified, freed itself from its historical roots, and finally lost its essence: the belief in the divinity of Jesus. He came back from China more preoccupied than ever with religious questions, but more of a theist than a Christian.

Apart from his Mandarin teacher, Jacques' initiators into Chinese culture were not Asians but enlightened Europeans. It was not a good period for Franco-Chinese friendship. After Chiang Kai-shek had established a nationalist government in Nanking in 1928, China had shut herself off from the West. The Kuomintang's program was aimed at reconstructing the country from the interior, developing the local economy, and protecting small workshops manufacturing local products—which implied blocking the entry of Western goods by introducing taxes and customs duties, refusing foreign merchant ships the right to coastal trading, and above all reclaiming the Chinese soil conceded to foreigners for more than fifty years. So the government reneged on the economic treaties signed with the Western powers, considering them inequitable, and fomented xenophobia to provide a scapegoat for the misery of the people, crushed by famine and banditry. Naturally, this protectionist policy intensified the rivalry between the British, French and U.S. companies on the spot, and French exporters were particularly disadvantaged because they specialized in luxury goods.

Even though he dreamed of it, de Prévaux was well aware that nobody could get to know China in just a few months. Yet, judging by his experiences in Berlin, he thought it might be possible for him to forge the same sort of trusting relationships with the Chinese elite as he had with the German employers and bankers. But he came under great pressure from French traders to defend their interests by diplomatic, or even military, means.

War had broken out between China and Japan. Pursuing its plans for expansion and westward conquest, Tokyo decided to annex China, and invaded Manchuria in September 1931. De Prévaux had taken command of the *Altaïr* three months earlier. Peking refused to negotiate, and Japan went on to attack China's economic and political heart: Shanghai. In January 1932 the vice admiral commanding the French fleet in the Far East was absent, and de Prévaux had replaced him. Liaising with the French authorities (the consul, the colonel and the police), he was in charge of France's response.

Naturally, there was no question of taking sides between the belligerents, even though France wasn't forgetting that China, in 1917, had rallied to the Allies' cause. Moreover, during the Washington Conference on the Pacific in 1922, the Western powers had called on Japan to put an end to her expansionist ambitions. Apart from these diplomatic decisions hostile to Japan, France had a prejudice in favor of China. "Judged as individuals, as artists, associates, or from the literary point of view," Jacques noted, "for us, the Chinese (perhaps also because they are even more mysterious) are much more sympathetic." And in the present conflict it was undeniable that "according to appearances, and even to reality, poor defenseless China had been violated and invaded in defiance of laws and treaties by a brutal, dishonest Japan, real Prussians of the Far East." Tokyo's contempt for the League of Nations was a further reason for criticizing the Japanese offensive, which Shanghai traders held responsible for the worst thing they could imagine: it brought business to a halt.

Should France therefore take the side of the Chinese? It wasn't so simple, Jacques thought. "However unpleasant it may seem to us, however antipathetic they may be or inept they may have been, the Japanese are now defending the cause of civilization in general and of French interests in particular." The advent of a nationalistic and xenophobic government had indeed changed the basic facts of the problem. They ought to hope for a Japanese victory, even if the prestige of the League of Nations were to suffer thereby, because the Japanese represented France's sole chance of saving its concessions, albeit if only for a short respite, as these privileges were in any case doomed to disappear. "A Chinese victory, or simply the absence of a Chinese defeat, would mean that Chinese anarchy would become established in the prosperous, well-ordered towns that are the pride of Europeans in China." This pro-Japanese analysis (in the name of French interests and not of any affinity with the "Prussians of the Far East") was not that of those who represented France in Shanghai. They were too much influenced by the relationships they had established with their Chinese friends, and by their memories of many pleasant years and so many works of art collected, to recognize lucidly that it was in France's interests to hope for the defeat of China.

Like Britain, for that matter, France had at first tried to act as an intercessor between the belligerents and had proposed her good offices to help them to come to some arrangement. These efforts were ruined by a new Japanese offensive, after which the only thing that remained was to try to protect the concessions, to see that the rights imposed by the Western powers were respected—in the first place the maintenance of the naval bases. And then, in the midst of the battles, to defend the zones of commercial influence and, as a last resort, to negotiate the evacuation of French nationals.

On the front, which extended from Wusong to south of Shanghai, the instructions to the navy were to protect the French concessions and the factories that depended on them, and to be ready to evacuate within an hour the personnel of these factories and the nuns from the convent. Immediately after the first Japanese ultimatum on January 28, 1933, de Prévaux set up a warning system, redeployed the naval units at his disposal, and released combat squads to support the defense of the concessions and factories. In the city itself, the greatest risk was that the local Chinese would be panicked into invading the French concession to seek refuge there. The consul joined the warning system set up by the other powers and had the concession surrounded by barbed wire—a measure, he realized, above all intended to reassure public opinion susceptible to the alarming news. However, the advance of the Japanese troops finally began to worry Westerners, who wondered how, under bombing, they could get the neutral status of the concessions respected, and who couldn't manage to negotiate an understanding between the belligerents.

In fact, the conflict between the twelve thousand Japanese and the forty thousand Chinese was to run its course without affecting the concessions. Having rejected a second ultimatum, and after several weeks of heavy artillery attacks, the final Japanese offensive was launched on February 20. That same day, the Japanese cavalry reached the Shanghai racecourse and made it their base of operations. The Chinese troops retreated—on January 31 Chiang Kai-shek had transferred the government capital from Nanking to Leyang—and on March 2 they accepted a ceasefire agreement according to which they had to retreat to a line 10 kilometers behind the front.

For Shanghai, the war was over. But the Japanese continued their conquest of China from Manchukuo, and were already marching on Peking.

Mao Tse-tung was still in Kiangsi Province, organizing a "Chinese Soviet Republic."

De Prévaux left the *Altaïr* in July 1933 and was taken home on the *Athos II*. He was entitled to four months' end-of-commission leave, which he spent in Italy with Blandine and their two daughters. It was early autumn. The de Prévaux traveled as well-to-do tourists between Florence, Siena and Pisa.

Tuscany was bathed in a light that Jacques, lost in admiration, tried to analyze: clarity, subtlety, delicacy .... He described the sublime landscapes in his diary, and pondered over the beautiful sights on the banks of the Arno and the village fêtes in Umbria. He knew Italy only from the few occasions when the *Duguay-Trouin* had put into port there and from the rare excursions organized by the training school when he was twenty. What he chiefly remembered was the frustration he had felt when the crew were not allowed to go ashore at some of the most beautiful sites of Roman history. This leisurely trip was a constant delight.

After a month of this cultural holiday, the children went

back to France for the start of the new year at their fashionable convent school, Les Oiseaux, while Blandine and Jacques drove to Rome in their Fiat. For Blandine, this was no longer tourism but work. She was writing a book on youth in Fascist Italy and had come to do research and conduct interviews. She had a tight schedule—just two weeks to gather enough material. She paid many visits to the Casa del Fascio, wrote articles about an orphanage, a home for abandoned children, a juvenile court, schools, and private establishments for girls. She managed to obtain several interviews with Count Ciano, whose father-in-law, Mussolini, had just made him undersecretary of state for the press and propaganda, and she even had the honor of meeting Il Duce in person. The result of all this was published by Gallimard the following year and entitled *Fascist Youth*. In between her extravagant descriptions of this youth, which was "vigorous, healthy and dynamic" and worked hard at school in order to please Il Duce, the author's admiration for Mussolini's achievements was clearly expressed.

During this time Jacques was exploring Rome. He spent hours walking through the city. He visited its churches and museums, lunched with various people, used his intuition, observed, and wrote. In the evenings, while dressing to go out to dinner, he would ask Blandine about her work and encourage her to carry on. "You need to work." He helped her find a secretary to type what she had already written. Rome's treasures cannot possibly be explored in one month, and it was with a heavy heart that he started for home.

Back in Paris under the driving rain of early November, things looked grim. The Olliviers accorded a frosty welcome to their son-in-law, whom they had still not forgiven for the Berlin scandal. Up till then Jacques and Blandine had been living with them, but they now decided to look for an apartment of their own. Jacques' leave was nearly over, and the list of available postings contained nothing of interest. Things were going badly.

* * *

And then one evening Charlotte Leitner, whom everyone
called Lotka, appeared before him—a figure dressed in black,
her very pale face surrounded by a mass of golden hair—and
conquered him with a single look from her green eyes.

PART II

LOTKA

7

FROM JAROSLAW TO VIONNET

On a January morning in 1934, Lotka Leitner took the Krakow-bound train. She had tucked her ticket safely away in her leather glove, the cardboard rectangle against her palm, and was clutching to her bosom the crocodile handbag that contained her most precious possession, her brand-new passport. Lotka had been French for just one month. How strange it is, she thought, burying her nose in the bunch of violets Mopse was holding out to her. She had waited so long for the moment when she would at last have her papers, when she would finally be French. Yet the first thing she was doing was going back to Poland and leaving her adored Paris, which she now felt was home. And yet she was so happy at the thought of being back in Poland, seeing her parents again, going skiing in the mountains, and enjoying the carefree holiday of an ordinary young woman.

Ordinary? Hardly. As she walked down the platform with a mannequin's swaying step, her tall figure (about five foot nine) swathed in furs, a mass of frothy blonde hair escaping from her modish hat, it was as if a perfumed breeze were passing by under the glass roof. She went on, and people stopped to follow her with their eyes; there was something indefinable about her that attracted their attention. Her charm lay in her long, supple neck which seemed to bend under the weight of her face with its wide Slavonic cheekbones; in the transparency of her enormous eyes whose subtle color turned blue, gray or green according to her mood, the weather, or the clothes she was wearing; in the sensuality of her wavy golden hair; in the grace and distinction of her movements. No one really noticed that her nose was too big, her mouth too wide, and her chin a little weak. She had become so used to the admiring glances that followed her everywhere that she barely noticed them. Modest, and at heart still untamed, she didn't realize how special she was. And anyway, at twenty-seven, she had no need to act the coquette; this mute admiration merely amused her. So she climbed the steps of the train laughing to herself, bestowed a dazzling smile of thanks on the kind man who hoisted her suitcase up into the carriage, and blew a last kiss with her gloved hand to Mopse, standing there on the platform sadly watching her go.

When they were saying good-bye that morning, Mopse had pretended to be unconcerned. She would be strong, she wouldn't cry and make a fool of herself. During the few weeks Lotka would be away she would go to Brussels and spend a week with her father, her "papaschka," whom she had recently been neglecting, and then go to Davos to keep René Crevel company. He was once again in one of those depressing sanatoriums that never managed to cure him of his tuberculosis. Mopse lived from one passion to another, and couldn't understand the indifference of this beautiful girl, who had never been in love. Eaten by jealousy, she imagined Lotka's irresistible charm reigning supreme during the evenings in Zakopane, the fashionable ski resort in the Tatra mountains. With a laugh, she had told her friend to be good.

Settling down in her compartment, Lotka on the contrary promised herself that she was going to enjoy herself. Antoine, who was more or less just a good friend, had sworn that he would try to join her in Zakopane. This well-to-do son of a banker was neither young nor attractive, but he had other qualities. He loved music and played the violin to perfection. The lavish lifestyle of a rich dilettante that he lived in Paris had an amazing appeal for the little émigrée she still was.

And yet, what a lot of changes there had been since she had jumped out of the Krakow train one December evening in 1924, eager to discover Paris! She was then eighteen and had very little luggage, but she had in her pocket an address that was worth its weight in gold: that of Reboux, one of the great Paris milliners. She was going there to improve her skills in putting the finishing touches to hats, an art that could be learned only in the luxury establishments of Paris. After that, she was to go back to Jaroslaw and practice her new talents in the family boutique. A fine shop, the most elegant in that little town in the south of Poland, whose signboard said it all: AU CHIC PARISIEN. It was the family business; the mother was in charge of the milliners' workshop, while the father managed the factory that made the felt.

Like so many Jews from central Europe, Lotka's parents had tried their luck at emigrating and sailed for New York. Exhausted and distressed by the crossing, they landed on Ellis Island, where they were herded together like cattle in a huge room and surrounded by armed Yankees. There, they submitted without complaint to the jostling of the waiting crowds and the humiliation of police checks and health examinations. The name of Leitner can be found among the others carved on a wall in Ellis Island, commemorating all the thousands of immigrants who arrived there. Lotka's father, Isidore, had left Poland first, found work on the railways, and sent for his wife and Milan, his firstborn. Lotka (Charlotte, according to her new French papers) was born and spent her early childhood in New York, on Avenue B, in the tumultuous, supercharged atmosphere of the Lower East Side, where diverse immigrant communities lived side by side. But the family never got used to it. It wasn't easy to leave a well-ordered bourgeois life, a quasi-rural and traditional milieu, for the hectic life of an industrial society and the barbarity of the poor districts in New York. Since they had not been fleeing poverty or pogroms, there was no reason for them not to go back to Poland. So, after six years of exile, Isidore repatriated his family to Jaroslaw.

Lotka's mother, Bertha, was a rather heavily built beauty, with a stern look and an ample bosom. She got down to work again, and won back her clientele in Jaroslaw by deploying her talents and, above all, her energies. This capable woman was following in her family's footsteps. Her mother, Rosa Stieglitz, was still famous in local memory. Admiring tales were told about how, one fine day, she had decided to take her family affairs in hand. Exasperated by the avarice of her husband, who was a watchmaker and ungodly (he dared to smoke on Saturdays, and gave up this sacreligious habit only after setting his bed on fire), she decided to make herself independent and became a midwife. Her daughter, Bertha, followed her up the social ladder by marrying Isidore Leitner and becoming the boss.

Although they were strictly orthodox Jews (they respected the Sabbath, and every morning Isidore conducted prayers wearing the phylacteries), they were middle-class and recognized as such—in short, they were socially acceptable. Jaroslaw, which until the First World War was part of the Austro-Hungarian Empire, had in any case been spared by the pogroms. The hats made by the skilled hands of Au Chic Parisien's workers were the most elegant in the whole town; if the wives of all the important citizens had not patronized it, they would have been ridiculed. Bertha was determined to keep up to date with the very latest fashions, and every year she visited those shrines of good taste, Vienna and Paris, and brought her latest discoveries back to her eager customers. The names of her finds, printed in the pages of the glossy magazines, set even the least vain of them dreaming: "Mon Flirt" (felt with a metal buckle), "Promenade des Anglais" (a little toque in a mottled gray and black tweed), or "Des Grieux" (a tricorne in black Baku).

Bertha also came back from her foreign travels with clothes for her daughter, her lovely Lotka, her pride and joy, so that she could be decently dressed. Dresses to go out in and dresses for Jaroslaw's elegant soirées. Lotka still remembered the pink chiffon gown she wore for her first ball, when she was sixteen. Her little brother Willy would always remember it: "She was radiantly beautiful!" She danced without a break, although she'd been afraid that her height might put her partners off. In those peaceful days before Nazism, she had a gilded youth, spent between piano lessons and balls—and her mother's workshop.

She had to work hard. There is a photo of the seamstresses, seven serious, rather tense-looking girls, each holding the hat she is engaged in making, grouped around their employer. Lotka is sitting on her mother's right; she is the only one looking at the camera with calm defiance. All Bertha's hopes were centered on her, as well as her hopes for the future of Jaroslaw's Au Chic Parisien and the family business. Lotka was a good apprentice, she had taste—which was only natural, of course, for someone in constant touch with Bertha—but more was needed if she was to be worthy of carrying on the tradition.

Evening after evening the mother laid siege to Isidore: their daughter had to go to Paris to learn what Parisian chic really was. She had managed to get her an apprenticeship with the capital's most famous milliner, Reboux, whose workshops in the avenue Matignon supplied the great couturiers. This would be a reference—better still, an honor. Naturally, the father raised a thousand objections. His beautiful Lotcienka, still so young, lost in the big city, exposed to the innumerable dangers of that pagan hell? And how would they live without her smile? And who would look after the three younger children still at home, Willy, Mania and Mina? Bertha, who knew how to travel all over Europe without difficulty, stuck to her guns, spoke of prestige, of profits, and reminded him that their eldest son, Milan, was already living in Paris and would be able to put the child up, seeing that it would only be for a few months.

In the end, Isidore gave in. But Lotka was going to stay in France, and it would be another ten years until the Leitners saw their daughter again. Not long afterwards, fleeing anti-Semitism, they too were to go to Paris, as refugees.

With a deafening squeal of brakes grating on the frozen rails and with a hiss of steam, the train finally pulled into the station in Krakow. Lotka's uncle, an old Talmud scholar, shivering as he tried to shelter from the snow flurries under the awning over the ticket windows, kept darting anxious glances at the few travelers hurrying toward the relative warmth of the building. All of a sudden his niece was there in front of him, but so transformed that he recognized her only by her height: a lady as tall as that could only be Lotka.

Karpel Leitner, her father's brother, lived in two dark little rooms above his leather goods workshop, in a steeply sloping street in the old town. Lotka, who had been revived by the fresh air and the forgotten but so familiar fumes of the smoke from the coke stoves, felt as if she were suffocating as she entered the little apartment with its musty smell of leather. Then, as soon as she had sat down in the shabby old armchair over which her uncle had thrown a multicolored blanket, the warmth made her feel drowsy again. She looked vaguely at the old man who, his eyes sparkling with curiosity, was waiting for her to tell him all about herself. She felt she was at the end of the world in this stuffy, isolated flat, where the street noises were muffled by the thick curtains, and even the jangling of the trams was deadened by the snow. So far from Paris, in any case, from her studio flat in the rue de Passy, from the luxurious atmosphere of the avenue Montaigne, from the excitement of the fashion parades.

* * *

When Lotka had first arrived in Paris, almost ten years before, she went to live with her brother, as agreed with her parents. But she didn't stay there long. He had welcomed her with open arms—family ties are sacred—but Lotka soon felt that he was embarrassed by the irruption of Jaroslaw into his Paris life. Milan had his work—he was a barrister, or at least a legal adviser— and it was awkward for him to have to put up this young Polish girl who could only stammer out a few words in French, with a strong Yiddish accent. He was about to be married, and Jeanne, his future wife, was reluctant to share her home with a younger woman, especially one who was so strikingly beautiful. Milan found his sister a room with the widow of a Greek diplomat. A perfect solution, although the avenue du Maine was a little far from the center, but it was a big room and the rent was moderate. Lotka would still have been there had the widow not had a son, the memory of whom still disgusted her. He was a layabout who hung around in the flat all morning, casually dressed in a fancy silk dressing gown; an oaf who always managed to be there when she passed by so as to inflict his witticisms on her; an arrogant fellow who blew the sweetish smoke of his oriental cigarettes in her face; a self-satisfied playboy who insisted on giving her a detailed account of his evening assignations and mocked her for being so reserved and shy. But she left immediately when his allusions became precise propositions and he tried to take advantage of her embarrassment. In no time she had packed her bag, and she took it with her when she went to work at Vionnet's in the avenue Montaigne.

After her apprenticeship with Reboux, the four years she spent with Madeleine Vionnet were pure pleasure, in spite of the hard work—the mannequins were on their feet all day, and always instantly available—and the insecurity of her situation. She was an illegal immigrant, since she had no work permit and her employer, who set great store by her, hid her whenever she heard that inspectors were on their way. The great couturiere could afford to take this risk; since everyone knew that she was otherwise on the right side of the law, these checks were a simple matter of form. Vionnet had created exceptionally good working conditions. The workshops were spacious and well lit, and comfortable too, as the apprentices had real chairs and not just stools. They had good salaries, and above all, they had a free canteen, four weeks' holiday, and an infirmary and a dental surgery where they were given free treatment. Vionnet's working girls would have gone to the stake for such an employer, and the forewomen happily spent their Sundays looking for new models, without earning an extra sou if they found one who was taken on.

How had Lotka managed to enter such a prestigious house? Her training period with Reboux had naturally brought her into contact with Vionnet, the principal client of the great modiste. While they are preparing their collections, couturiers work closely with their accessories suppliers. In haute couture, hats, gloves and shoes were then an essential part of their creations. No woman would ever have gone out without a hat, and in the pages of *Vogue* the models always called attention to all the elements of an outfit. It may have been one of Vionnet's staff who noticed the girl's striking beauty, or a delighted customer may have mentioned her to Madeleine Vionnet.

Even in this wealthy district, the procession of Rolls-Royces and Bugattis calling at 50 avenue Montaigne drew attention to Maison Vionnet's magnificent mansion. A monumental staircase led up to the grand salon, where the collections were presented. Everywhere there was an atmosphere of refinement created by the antique-style frescoes, the light filtered through the Lalique stained-glass windows, the thick carpets, the fitting rooms with their moiré silk walls, the sumptuous contents of the glass cabinets in the lingerie and fur salons. Behind, a five-story building housed the twenty-odd couture workshops, one for loose-fitting garments, another for furs, others for *chichis*—frills and ruffles—where they ironed the ribbons and made the silk or velvet roses. The ostentatious luxury of the Maison Vionnet deeply impressed Lotka at first; she was almost trembling with fright when a dress being designed for a client was for the first time made up on her, one of those evening gowns cut on the bias for which Vionnet was famous, which had such a natural flow that they seemed simple but were in fact complicated. The white silk clung to her shapely figure, while her slightest movement set the delicate material in motion. A shameless garment, Lotka thought, and its harsh contact with her naked skin made her shudder. But then, turning to look at herself in the long mirror, she discovered the elegance of the gown. The dresser's approving look completed her metamorphosis, and she ungratefully repudiated the pink dress she had worn to her first ball.

With her tall, slender figure, Lotka was very different from the type of model usually chosen by Madeleine Vionnet for her fashion shows. One of her favorites was a buxom, redheaded beauty, Antoinette. And yet the brilliant couturiere liked to create her dresses on Lotka, draping the material here, pinning it there, adding something loose and flowing, her hands unhesitatingly accomplishing the look she had imagined, for at Vionnet's the designs were confirmed only after they had been tried out first on a wooden dummy and then on flesh-and-blood mannequins. When Lotka left, her employer wrote her a reference saying, "Her departure deprives me of one of the girls I most like to create my designs on and I deeply regret it."

After four years of extremely hard work in the fashion house, Lotka had decided to leave Vionnet. She had no complaints about her employers or about the other girls. Everyone was nice. At first, modest as she was, she had been shocked by the intimacy of the overheated cubicles where half-naked girls had to await a client's whim before getting into extravagant finery, and also by the laughter and complicity among the pretty young women. Later, she saw that she had found the affection there that it was useless to expect from brutes like the son of her former landlady. But once the thrill of the early days had worn off, the hushed, confined atmosphere, dedicated to luxury, began to weigh on her; it was too artificial for the wild young woman she had remained. It was time for her to learn a real profession, to obtain valid papers so that she could work normally and not be afraid of being expelled—in short, for her to establish herself permanently in France. She went to work for Elizabeth Arden.

In Karpel Leitner's room, the tea had got cold. Hoarse from having talked so much, all Lotka could think of was sleep. Her uncle, already so proud of the beautiful girl his niece had become, nodded with delight. So she was French now; that's an honor for our race. And that new profession, beautician, was that a good thing? And she hadn't said a word about her little brother Willy, although he was also in Paris. Didn't they see one another? Bertha's three eldest children were now in France— well done! We shall go, too; life is getting hard here for our people.

The next day Lotka took the train again, a wretched rattle-trap that puffed its way up the 100 kilometers between Krakow and Zakopane. The journey was grueling. The train was packed; the skiers' coarse jackets gave off an acrid smell of damp wool; the condensation on the windows blurred the view of the Tatra mountains. But the moment she got out onto the wooden platform of the tiny station, she rediscovered the dazzling, snowy scenery, the icy sky, and the tang in the air that she had been missing.

The Pension Granit was a modest lodging house where her cosmopolitan air and elegant clothes seemed out of place. But what did that matter, since she would mostly be out on the slopes. A good skier, rapid and tireless, she was very soon surrounded by the champions of the resort. As always, a masculine court established itself around her, magnetized by her smile and her joie de vivre. The group became inseparable, whether assembled with their rucksacks outside the chalets, strolling in town clothes in the streets of Zakopane, where a local photographer caught her (the elegant Parisienne in her waisted, tailor-made suit with a fur collar, matching muff and high-heeled ankle boots), or dining in evening dress. Looking radiant and tanned, she could be seen at a restaurant wearing a very low-cut black gown.

Paris, and her work as a demonstrator for Elizabeth Arden, seemed a long way away. From time to time she found a melancholy card from Mopse waiting for her at the pension. The poor darling implored her, "Come back quick, and whatever you do, don't deceive me." On one postcard, Mopse drew a picture of herself counting the days and even the hours, with a very red heart that was at Zakopane with a pretty skier.... Mopse had a real talent for drawing and made two lovely charcoal sketches of Lotka.

Lotka was touched by these love letters and wrote to her often. But she wasn't going to allow anything to spoil her carefree holiday.

Not even her letters from Jacques de Prévaux.

8

CONQUEST BY CORRESPONDENCE

Lotka had met him a month before, at Mopse's, one rainy evening in November 1933. Yet there had been little likelihood that the paths of the commander and the humble beautician, however beautiful, would ever cross.

At that time Lotka was spending almost every evening with Mopse, and she sometimes stayed the night. Her friend Ruth had finally introduced her to the celebrated Mopse, whose eccentricities were on everyone's lips. This same Ruth had just come back from Cannes, where Mopse had treated her like a princess in the most splendid luxury hotels. Mopse's scandalous reputation had reached Vionnet's: one of Lotka's fellow mannequins was a member of the club of opium-smokers to which Mopse belonged. In her turn, Lotka had become fascinated by the young German woman, a whirlwind of life and passions, and she admired, without really understanding, the fact that, at the same time and with equal sincerity, Mopse could constantly fall in love and yet remain faithful to the two men in her life: the writer René Crevel, to whom she had at one time been engaged, and the painter Carl von Ripper, whom she had married in 1929. Crevel had also been smitten with him, and they entered into a ménage à trois, a bizarre succession of visits to homosexual bars and opium dens alternating with sojourns in salubrious Swiss sanatoriums.

One November evening, Lotka was at Mopse's when a visitor rang the doorbell. "This is an old friend from Berlin," Mopse told her as she performed the introductions. Jacques, back in Paris after his Far Eastern service, had come to renew his acquaintance. Since their time there, where they had received René Crevel and his companion Mopse, the de Prévaux had continued to see them. As Crevel was almost always in Switzerland they saw even more of Mopse, who was also a friend of Gide and Eluard, and who moved in the literary circles they frequented. Actually, Lotka didn't hear much of the conversation. She was trying to shake off the effect of his burning gaze, which both embarrassed and unsettled her.

Lotka and Jacques hadn't had time to see much of each other. But the few occasions on which they did meet allowed them to get to know each other a little, and to realize that they had a great deal in common. They went to concerts, talked about books, and promised to meet when Lotka came back from Poland. She knew little about Jacques. He was a handsome man in the prime of life, with a fascinating smile, a charmer whom you didn't forget once you'd met him, and whom you wanted to see again. His eyes, in particular, made a profound impression, as did his way of looking right into you, making you feel unique. But there was something more, which puzzled her. During the long day she spent on the train between Paris and Krakow, she often thought about him, perplexed at not knowing what sort of person she was dealing with. A ladies' man, accustomed to making easy conquests? No doubt about that, it was obvious by the way he had seemed to think that women would automatically fall into his lap. And yet she had felt there was a kind of austerity about him, a reserve that belied the first impression and aroused her curiosity. He was totally different from everyone she knew.

The young Polish woman had developed during the nine years she had lived in Paris. Her French was impeccable (apart from a slight accent, which everyone thought adorable), and Milan and Jeanne had opened the doors of French society to her. Jeanne was a journalist, and Lotka met writers and critics at their flat. She was shy at first, but became more assured, and joined in their conversations with some success. André Malraux, among others, made vague advances to her; one evening at the Brasserie Lipp he grabbed hold of her hand and flamboyantly claimed to read her future in it. Then he paled and refused to say anything. When she went to powder her nose, he told Jeanne that her sister-in-law would come to a tragic end. Lotka discovered that she felt very much at ease in this literary world. She signed up for courses at the Faculty of Arts at the Sorbonne and acquired the culture she lacked. She was especially fond of poetry. With disconcerting facility she wrote pages of impeccable alexandrines in the then fashionable style of Paul Géraldy.

So Jacques and she found that they had tastes in common, the same liking for literature and for long discussions on art, happiness, the meaning of life—but with a seriousness new to her, which was in strong contrast to the fashionable conversations that went on in Jeanne's salon. The day before Lotka left for Poland, Jacques insisted on her putting three or four of his favorite books in her suitcase and seemed to set great store by her opinion. She was flattered by these signs of his interest, but from there to being in love . . . For it was indeed a question of love—imperious and urgent—from the very beginning, and Lotka wasn't ready. She valued her freedom.

Jacques' letters disturbed her. Hoping to be left in peace, she had not given him her address at the Pension Granit, and merely said something vague about the poste restante in Zakopane. She had no idea then that he was going to inundate so many Polish post offices—Krakow, Zakopane, Jaroslaw, Warsaw—with feverish daily letters. The first one she went to collect, between skiing runs, pleased her. "It's always nice to know that you're loved," she wrote to him. Her brief reply triggered a torrent of passionate, impatient letters, always asking the same questions: "Do you love me? Are you going to love me?" Even before she had got into the train he was already expecting a letter: "At your first stop, in Vienna, write me the words that will make me less frantic." Jacques, inflamed by his passion, demanded everything—demanded too much. He sometimes realized this and pretended a contrition that he didn't feel: "I feel bad at importuning you like this, at imposing myself on you so insistently"—only to cry out a few days later, "How can you go so long without writing to me?"

In the end, he did become importunate. They had spent only a few evenings together, she had promised him nothing, what right had he to pursue her all the way to Zakopane? After all, she was free! She didn't write another line. And anyway, she didn't have time, she was busy from morning to night. And when he carried his obstinacy to the extreme of sending her a telegram (reply paid!): WIRE ME IF RECEIVING LETTERS. GRIEVED SILENCE. I LOVE YOU, she replied with a curt: LETTERS RECEIVED. MINE FOLLOWS. VERY TOUCHED, and went off to join her cohort of admirers.

It was in Jaroslaw that Lotka began to weaken.

For Jacques had gone on writing, and she was obliged to collect her letters from the post office. Gradually, she too had become impatient. She would rip open the envelope in the snowy street without even taking off her gloves and unfold the two or three sheets covered in cramped handwriting—there were even some lines written sideways in the margin. She felt trapped by these words of love, these adoring phrases: "You are EVERY-THING that justifies my existence; all my confused desires, my chaotic aspirations are concentrated in you; I am no longer anything, I can no longer be anything more than an impassioned desire for you." Trapped, too, by his supplications: "I am eaten up with anxiety. What sort of cruel ordeal have you condemned me to, then? When are you going to allow me to hope again?" And also by his promises: "I shall talk to you in gentle, solemn words which will pierce you to the depths of your soul. . . . I promise you a great and glorious life, we shall be carried away by the passionate feeling that we are living on the heights, up among the soft breezes, far above mediocrities, banal joys, wretched pleasures and humiliated destinies."

Day after day she was smothered in tenderness, swathed in declarations of love, enveloped in hymns to her beauty. Whether she wrote him three banal words or remained silent, he turned either to his advantage and indulged in the tragic accents of the great passions. Everything she did he interpreted as a sign of love. Imperceptibly, she had become trussed up in silken threads like the prey of a spider. How could she resist this gentle encirclement?

Yet she tried desperately to defend herself. Her easygoing life suited her, she wanted to remain unattached. To be free to go out with Natasha, Mopse, or anyone else, to play the fool in lesbian bars, to dance, to listen to jazz in fashionable cellars, to meet people, to be courted—until now this had been all she wanted. A few unimportant affairs had given her the idea that love was a pleasant, transitory feeling. She realized that other ways of loving existed but, thank God, she had so far been spared a great love, an all-consuming, exclusive passion; she had naïvely promised herself that she would never fall in love. And Jacques' extravagant words ("I bless the suffering you are going to cause me") confirmed her in her decision. This violence frightened her. Her whole being rejected it.

But at the same time, all these affectionate letters had finally aroused something deeply hidden in her. And what if it were true, that sort of love, that bliss of becoming one with another person? All of a sudden there was only one thing she wanted: to be back in Paris and to see Jacques again to make sure of what his instinct was telling him, and also, quite simply, to throw herself into his arms and never leave him. It was obvious, clear and definite. As if a curtain had just fallen, her holiday had suddenly lost its value, Poland had suddenly become dull and boring. She wished she were already back in Paris. She did stay another few days in Jaroslaw with her parents but decided to cut out her visit to Warsaw.

It was a new Lotka who took the train once again. Jacques had laid siege to her by means of letters, he had conducted his campaign to win her by correspondence, and she arrived back in Paris completely conquered.

Both of them were trembling with joy and terror. Jacques was in a panic. Lotka had written to him: "The moment is approaching when I am going to love you" — an understatement, no doubt. But after that, nothing. Was she regretting her confession? He went from exaltation to despair. He was convinced that Lotka's first glance would decide his fate. He couldn't sleep. This was February 1934, and riots were breaking out all over Paris. He passed through them like a sleepwalker, seeing them merely as one more reason for him to dedicate his life to his love. In a fever, he looked back on his life: he was forty-five, but still well preserved, and in all humility he was going to make a gift to Lotka of everything he had accumulated. Yes, he was worthy of her. His dream was hardly clouded by Blandine's return to Paris with the children, even though it did slightly complicate things, in that Lotka wouldn't be able to telephone him at home.

And if she loved him — ah! if she loved him! How could he face the demands of such a passion? He knew how difficult it was for him to express his deepest feelings — he, the womanizer whose seductive gaze not even the prettiest of women could resist. But he now discovered how diffident he really was. The magic words, the outbursts of feeling, the lyricism with which he had covered page after page—he could never have brought himself to express them tête-à-tête.

When Lotka got out of the train at the Gare de l'Est, Jacques was on the platform, pale and distraught. They were hardly to have time to embrace, though, to whisper that they loved each other, for good and for life, before Jacques, finally appointed as station commanding officer, had to leave for a two-year stint in Rochefort.

Jacques de Prévaux age 12, Lille (1901).

Sublieutenant
Jacques de Prévaux (1915).

Jean Roulier, Toulon (1915).

On the *Descartes,* Montreal (1913). Sublieutenant
Jacques de Prévaux is seated on the left.

The *Descartes* (1913).

The crew of the *Diligente* (1916). Sublieutenant Jacques de Prévaux is seated in the second row, third from the left.

Jacques de Prévaux in airship pilot's flying gear, Saint-Cyr (1917).

Lieutenant Jacques de Prévaux, commander of the Marquise-Rinxent air base (September 1919).

Jacques de Prévaux and Blandine Ollivier at Saint-Augustin on their wedding day (April 1920).

Office of the Minstry of Defense,
Paris (1920). Lieutenant Jacques de
Prévaux is fourth from the right.

On the *Diligente*, Toulon (1924).
Captain Jacques de Prévaux is seated.

Captain Jacques de Prévaux (seated center), commander of the Cuers base (November 1924).

The *Esperia* landing at Cuers (1925).

Commander Jacques de Prévaux, naval attaché in Berlin (1929).

On the *Altaïr,* Shanghai (1931). Jacques de Prévaux (seated front row center) in command.

Jacques de Prévaux, China (1932).

Jacques de Prévaux with the commanding officer of American forces in the Philippines, Manila (1932).

The Leitners in New York
(1906). From left to right:
Bertha (holding Lotka),
Milan and Isidore.

Bertha Leitner's shop,
Au Chic Parisien,
Jaroslaw (1923).
Bertha Leitner is
second from the right;
Lotka is on her right.

Mannequin (thought to be Lotka) at Vionnet's.

MUSÉE DE LA MODE ET DU TEXTILE, COLL. UFAC. GIFT OF MADELEINE VIONNET, 1952

Lotka (1930s).

Postcard from Mopse to
Lotka (1934).

Lotka, Zakopane
(January 1934).

Lotka (1930s).

Jacques (1930s).

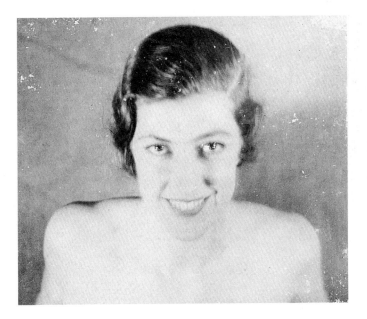

Lotka (1930s).

Letters from Jacques to Lotka (left) and
from Lotka to Jacques (right).

Jacques de Prévaux (1936).

Jacques de Prévaux talking to Admiral Castex, Rochefort (May 1936).

Souvenir photograph of Commander Jacques de Prévaux, Alexandria (September 1940).

The *Duguay-Trouin*, 1940

Lotka's false identity card in the name of Jacqueline Marie Chebrou (January 1942).

Lotka at La Cisampo (1942).

Isidore and Bertha Leitner outside their shop at 78 rue Legendre, Paris (1938).

Letter from Isidore Leitner to Lotka (September 1942).

"...Now, I must tell you how happy I am that you, my dearest children, I mean you and my dear Jacques, have saved my children [Lotka's sister, Mania, and her husband Kouba] from the wreck."

Bertha Leitner's last
postcard from Drancy
(March 1, 1943).

Lotka at La Cisampo (1942).

Jacques (1943).

Jacques de Prévaux's DSO certificate
(January 1943).

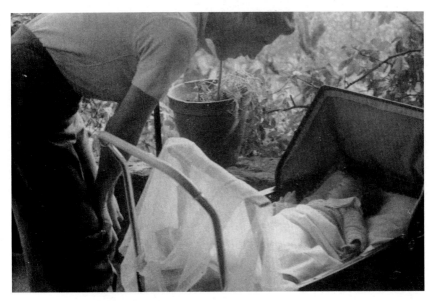

Lotka with Aude (1943).

Certificate for Lotka de Prévaux's Polish decoration, the Croix de Mérite (April 1945).

Lotka with Aude (1943).

9
ROCHEFORT

After eight years spent first in Berlin and then in China, de Prévaux was back with the Naval Air Service. At Cuers-Pierrefeu, he had been in command of a base where airships still had their part to play, though the service was already beginning to develop other kinds of aircraft: seaplanes and carrier-based planes. In 1934, Rochefort was the last base to use airships. It had half a dozen *vedettes* and escort-duty airships, and prototypes of semi-rigids. It was especially a training center for airship officer pilots—the last of them received their certificates in 1936—and also for non-officer personnel: ground crew and air engineers.

Jacques was delighted to be back in the familiar, heterogeneous setting of the Naval Air Service—the Picketty hangars and the other gigantic buildings made to house the airships, their forecourts, the hydrogen factories, the gasometers, the piping, the radio station, the airships' mooring mast. . . . And the typical sounds of dirigibles getting ready for takeoff: the thudding of the clogs of the two hundred sailors in the shunting gang, summoned by the bugle and rushing to get the gondola out of the hangar and hold it down on the ground until the commander gave the order "Let go!" and the cold shower of the ballast falling on them among their stifled oaths, and finally the calm, barely perceptible swish of the *peau de vache* (cowhide) gently rising into the skies.

These *peaux de vache*—the affectionate term for the dirigibles on account of their thick yellowish rubber envelopes—had for the most part given some fifteen years of good and loyal service, which proved how sturdy they were. In Rochefort, moreover, "revolutionary" prototypes were being tested, as for instance the V-11 and V-12 *vedettes* commanded by Sub-lieutenant de Brossard. He was to be the last airship pilot, and his V-12, a streamlined, trefoil-shaped dirigible 50 meters long, was to make its last sortie in 1937. Jacques piloted this particularly rapid and sensitive machine several times; it was the highest-performance model ever used by the French Navy, but it had no successor.

Admiral de Brossard always remained grateful to de Prévaux, who supported his efforts to get permission from the authorities to fly his prototypes. Unlike the engineers, who took the admiral for a dreamer, de Prévaux paid attention when he presented his inventions. He defended his men and, a rarer quality in a base commander, did not feel obliged to curb their spirit of adventure. De Brossard remembered, for instance, how understanding de Prévaux had been after a memorable escapade with a free balloon. It was in February 1935: caught in a storm, the craft, with a crew of five men, had landed somewhat dramatically near Béthune after a seven-hour flight. De Brossard, the pilot, was guilty of having persisted in going up despite forecasts of bad weather. De Prévaux went to Paris to plead his cause and wrote an indulgent report: "Excess of sporting spirit, very excusable in young officers."

But airships were on their way out. The navy now preferred carrier-based planes, and especially seaplanes. More and more prototypes were being created, and daring aviators went up in machines that were still unreliable, and crossed Africa and the oceans. Nungesser and Coli, Costes and Le Brix, Bonnot and

Mermoz took off on test flights in seaplanes specially built for the Naval Air Force. At the Rochefort base, pilots trained on planes as varied as the very successful and popular Potez-25s, the CAMS-37 (biplanes with hulls, the same model as the one that flew from Berre and Saint-Louis-du-Sénégal in 1926), the FBA-17s. They even tested a bizarre machine called an autogyro, which in the end was never developed but is considered to be an ancestor of the helicopter. Naturally, the commander of the base took to the air less frequently than the pilots, since he had other duties, but Jacques enjoyed making it his business to take his turn in flying these numerous planes—a completely different exercise from handling a balloon or an airship.

De Prévaux, then, was overworked. There were more than a thousand men at the base, whom he had to command and inspire. There were the committees to chair, the advisory meetings with aircraft designers to organize, the inspections, the reports to write, the troops to review. In a single morning, he proudly noted, he had received seventeen visitors, established the forty-hour week, held an inspection, written ten reports and signed a hundred and fifty papers. His orderly, meticulous mind drove him always to do more than was strictly necessary. He had an obsessive fear of leaving undone something that could have been done. The head of his secretarial staff declared that "it became a real pleasure to see all the outstanding matters dealt with in the minimum time." But he was in his element—he was born to command. Having always found it difficult to show his feelings, he was now quite naturally able to establish contact with his men, to make them feel his authority and his goodwill at the same time. Reputed to be a slave driver, he could indeed demand a great deal, but his understanding attitude made the strict discipline easier to take. The most severe inspections seemed less terrifying when they were carried out by a commander who had a hand in his pocket. "That made us warm to him," said Camille Migaud, one of the ground crew.

Everyone felt his charisma. When he left, the men gave him "most unusual evidence of their affection."

In addition to his actual work, he had the social obligations of officers in a garrison town, where life is carefully organized around more or less obligatory activities: cultural (concerts, touring theater companies, cinemas) and sporting (tennis, shooting); charities; bourgeois rites like the weekly bridge game; and "informal" dinners. If we add the compulsory support of the events organized by the flying club, the unavoidable ceremonies such as the speeches at the Rochefort lycée's prize-givings, the crew's annual party with games and a ball, and the receptions in honor of the admiral on a tour of inspection, we can see that Jacques' social life was more than full. He performed these duties with ease and courtesy. On his departure, the local paper devoted a column to regretting the loss of: "This affable, reserved man of taste, this fine scholar, whose natural distinction is revealed in his manner, his language and his spirit.... The municipal authorities and the town's other notabilities are fortunate in the relationships they have had with him, and have nothing but praise for the tact of which he has always given proof."

In Rochefort, the de Prévaux lived in a pleasant villa with a garden and led a more or less normal family life. Their daughters, who were nine and thirteen, finally had their father with them. They still had their governess to look after them, the faithful "Miss," who had come into the family to take care of their mother when she was a baby and who never left them, even to take a holiday. As for Blandine, she was bored to death in this little provincial town. She had nothing in common with the other officers' wives, and she found the navy's social gatherings, which she was expected to frequent, an unbearable chore. She played the piano, finished her book on Mussolini, and escaped as often as possible to Paris, where she met her close woman friend Charly.

This picture of a happy family was a facade. Jacques and Blandine had already drifted apart when they were in Berlin, and the relationship between father and daughters was affected by the reserve from which Jacques suffered. And above all, there was Lotka.

10
A DOUBLE LIFE

Jacques was always thinking of her. Known as a workaholic, he amazed the rear admiral by claiming all the leave he was entitled to and rushing off to Paris to spend it in Lotka's arms. A few days of bliss, which they had been dreaming of for three months. As the date grew nearer, Jacques would grow so excited that he couldn't sleep and Lotka felt faint. If his leave was canceled or postponed, her despair was so intense that it worried him.

When he was with her, the stern commander became happy, young, more so than he had ever been, even lighthearted. He took an interest in fashion, in dancing, in poetry—in frivolous pursuits. He was forty-six, but he told her he was only forty. The lie must have been believable, because Lotka proudly reported to him that her girlfriends thought he was only thirty-five. He had been inhibited by an education that distrusted sensitivity and condemned the flesh, and had withdrawn into himself under the capital-letter pressure of Moral Values and a Sense of Duty. Their love released him from some of his feelings of shame, and gave him the confidence in himself that a series of affairs had never done. Happy at last, he relaxed and blossomed. He loved and was loved for the first time in his life.

Then, sadly, he would take the train back to Rochefort. No sooner had the door closed than the Lotka who had been so cheerful and amusing went out like a candle, transformed into a distraught woman who collapsed in tears of despair, incapable of living without Jacques. And he, no sooner had he reached the bottom of her staircase than he had already put a love letter in her mailbox. He would post another at the station and then, in the train, he would once again write her bewitching, soothing words: "We are going to extend the limits of human love!" During his two years in Rochefort they had not been able to live together for more than three days here or there, a week at Easter, two weeks during the summer, and a few more days again in the autumn.

They lived on words of love, on heartrending letters and crazy telegrams. A day without a letter caused panic, a letter that was too short was anguish. Jacques was always on the lookout for the postman. He would delay exercises until the mail had been delivered, and the beautiful ceremony of the blessing of the sea seemed interminable to him because he had a retired admiral on his hands and not a second alone to read Lotka's letter. But he gave everything he had to his work, so he was better able than she to bear their separation. He was also the more intellectual of the two, and found a certain satisfaction in writing to his beloved daily. But Lotka was fragile, and the alternation of happiness and despair was too much for her nerves. Her work as a demonstrator for Elizabeth Arden was tedious; gossip and backbiting surrounded her. The office would send her to Marseille just when Jacques was coming to Paris—and worse, he was fiercely jealous. She couldn't understand why he didn't get a divorce, and lost faith in his declarations of love and promises of a happiness that was always in the future. One February evening she went down to post a last cry for help (would he again reply with his fine phrases, or would he at last come and live with her?) and swallowed two tubes of sleeping tablets.

Jacques was terrified of losing her. "If we have to go, we'll go together, in each other's arms," he wrote, "but let us live first, and after our death, because even if we die a natural death a long time in the future, we shall die together, I know it, we shall be united forever in the cycle of rebirth in which my Buddhist soul believes." But Jacques finally realized that his words were no longer enough for Lotka to live by, that the silky cocoon he wove around her every evening could no longer protect her against her death wish. *His* one wish was never to have to leave her again, and as he had nearly come to the end of his time in Rochefort, he began to look for a posting in Paris.

It shouldn't have been too difficult to find an appointment worthy of his qualities, and to which his excellent service record entitled him. Admiral Walser, who was in command of the navy at Rochefort, had, like all de Prévaux's superior officers, noted on his record: first-rate officer. Given his age and his career, the choice was obvious: Staff College—*le Centre des hautes études navales* (CHEN)—which people accurately called "the School for Admirals." Every year this prestigious institute provided a dozen "auditors"—the most brilliant senior officers—with the overall strategic view that enabled them to earn their stars. So Jacques applied for a place. As he wrote to Admiral Darlan, the Chief of Naval General Staff: "Since the vicissitudes of my career have for so long kept me away from the fleet and from naval theory, nothing could be more opportune for me than to receive this instruction." He stressed that he had the necessary qualities for organizational posts in the upper echelons of the staff, in which he would be able to serve the navy most efficiently. His application was supported by his immediate chief, Admiral Walser, by Admiral Castex, and by the previous minister of the navy, François Pietri, whose successor, Senator Gasnier-Duparc, would also look favorably on him.

The only problem was that at forty-eight he was over the age limit—one more reason, his chiefs argued, to give new impetus to his exceptionally brilliant career (lieutenant-commander at thirty-five, commander at thirty-nine), which seemed to have got stuck since then. Vague rumors made Jacques afraid that some of the incidents in his past—opium-smoking during the war, the unfortunate incident in Berlin—might be hindering his advancement, but he was assured that these were just peccadilloes that had been completely forgotten. On the other hand, he discovered that in China Admiral Berthelot had not praised him as highly as might have been hoped. He had found him "pretentious," and had so described him in black and white in his file. Berthelot, in fact, had criticized de Prévaux for having differed from him in his analysis of the relative strengths of the Chinese and Japanese forces. After a frank discussion, the minister and Admiral Darlan did justice to de Prévaux and by dispensation, because of his age, appointed him an auditor at the CHEN. After a probation period in July 1937, he would be promoted to captain and admitted without problem as an auditor for the year 1937–38 to the *Collège des hautes études de défense nationale* (School of National Defense), which was the natural continuation of the "School for Admirals."

The sessions at these institutes were held in Paris but were preceded by courses of practical instruction. In the autumn of 1936 de Prévaux rejoined his home base of Toulon and spent several weeks there organizing and commenting on night exercises in coastal defense, submarine crossings, gunnery and torpedoing, and seaplane flights. He had been right to want to join the CHEN. From his very first day on the course he had recognized his ignorance in the essential field of the theory of defense and that his notions of tactics were very much out of date. And while he was familiar with the new form of defense, aviation, it was more as a pilot than as a strategist. Of course he had excuses; for the last ten years his assignments in Berlin and China had kept him away from France and oriented him more toward diplomacy, active service and the command of a base. But he was now mixing with officers of his own rank who knew more than he did, a completely new situation—he had always been top of his class—and mortifying to his pride.

Jacques worked like a slave to fill in the gaps in his knowledge. When the day's work was over, his body tired by the hectic pace of the exercises and lectures, his head full of new ideas, he would take a pile of papers to his room and spend part of the night studying them. He wanted to be the best. As a child he had already promised himself "to live and love only on the heights." He was now very conscious of his worth, and all the more proud in that he attributed all the credit for his success to himself; his family and his background had nothing to do with what he had become. "My mind, my intelligence, my value, whatever there is in me that is noble and proud, all belong to me in my own right." So he had to be first, to preserve his self-esteem, to prove to his superiors that they were right to have confidence in him, and to ensure that Lotka would be proud of him. And also, because the Trolley de Prévaux were always first in everything. Anyway, he had told Daniéla, his elder daughter, when she first went to school, "Given who your parents and grandparents are, you must always be among the top three."

In Paris, where the auditors of the "School of Admirals" met on the avenue Octave-Gréard, the work was less exhausting. The courses on strategy ("The Dardanelles Expedition"), on applied tactics ("Night attacks by torpedo boats"), and on the gases used in war, were even quite interesting. The auditors attended a great many lectures, such as the one given by Vice Admiral Castex, soberly entitled "From Genghis Khan to Stalin, or the vicissitudes of a strategic maneuver." Moreover, de Prévaux was delighted to see that his efforts had borne fruit when he was congratulated on the lecture he himself gave when his turn came, and he spoke on "The evolution of the German Navy's strategic plan from 1914 to 1918; its link with general strategy."

Finally, and above all, he was near Lotka. He could see her every day and bombard her with *pneus,* those tiny little letters sent by pneumatic tube, which arrived within an hour. At that rate, he could write to her several times a day. . . . At the beginning he led the classic double life of a married man with a mistress without too many scruples; he would escape in the evenings from the quai de Passy and sometimes wouldn't go back all night.

But Lotka wasn't happy. She was too sincere to be willing to share Jacques, too passionate to be satisfied with a few hours stolen from his wife and family. After May 1937 she had no work and soon became overwhelmed by financial worries. Her parents had been in exile in Paris for the previous few years and were living in poverty; their gas had just been cut off because they couldn't pay the bill. She worried herself sick at her inability to help them and couldn't expect anything from Jacques, who had no private income and had to keep his wife and children on his naval pay. Lotka's mother, Bertha, the energetic Jaroslav proprietress of the Au Chic Parisien, bore exile, deprivations and the hectic pace of life in the capital without complaint. The Leitners were courageous people whose motto might have been *Never say die*. But Bertha was grieved to see her daughter fading away. She was still beautiful, oh yes, but she looked so ill, and so pitiably sad. . . . Her unhappy love affair was to blame, of course, but their beautiful child was too good for that married man who could never make up his mind to get a divorce. Really, Lotka was wasting her time with him. There were so many other men who could make her happy.

Happy with someone other than Jacques? Impossible, inconceivable, Lotka protested with all her being. And anyway, happy or not, since one evening in November 1933 — already four years ago! — her destiny had been linked to Jacques'. She knew it. Then it all became too much for her: spending her days in her studio apartment in the Latin Quarter, staring stupidly at Jacques' photos pinned on the walls; always waiting — not for his letters, now, but for him in person—and a single look from him would make her melt with love and forget her doubts; always collapsing in sobs because he had gone again; always being told to be patient; always suffering too much. She decided to break with him. She wasn't tired of him—how could she be? She hadn't stopped loving him. It was simply that her mental health was at risk. She would travel, go back to the United States, go back to Poland, to Zakopane. Thank God she still had friends who would be only too happy to have her back! Maybe in time she would forget him. . . . In any case, no letters. And to show him that she was serious, she returned his.

Utterly distraught, Jacques acquiesced, and promised not to try to get in touch with her. He managed it for three months, wandering about like a madman, spending whole nights under Lotka's windows. He couldn't bear being away from her; the very idea of never seeing her again was intolerable. He told himself for the nth time that they had to be patient and wait until Blandine agreed to the divorce. He had first mentioned it to her when they were still living in Rochefort; she had alternated between threats (to ruin his career and his honor) and entreaties, reminded him that he hadn't a sou of his own, and held out for two years. But nothing could get Jacques to go back to her, and nothing could alienate him from his mistress.

From his mistress, or, even more contemptuously, from "that creature"—which was how some members of the family referred to Lotka. "A woman with neither country nor faith, her only asset her body, a vulgar nonentity, pure putrefaction," hissed one old aunt, herself no doubt a model of virtue. Another tried to get her nephew to return to the straight and narrow path of the moral laws, that's to say of discreet liaisons. "I know very well that you are not a saint (which didn't much matter) but what a coward you are!" (It was a little difficult to follow her logic.) Basically, they all considered that poor Jacques had been taken in and become the victim of the "infamy of a woman who is neither of your race nor of your religion, and is totally lacking in any moral sense, since she didn't scruple to bewitch you to such an extent." The more moderate among them preferred to believe that Jacques was ill. How could this scandalous divorce be explained if not by bewitchment or illness, the paranormal or the pathological?

The only one who understood Jacques was his cousin Roland de Margerie. At first amused and intrigued by this new liaison, he was amazed to discover how long it had lasted, realized that this time it was love, and was distressed by his cousin's mental and physical state. Would he dare go as far as divorce? Roland envied and admired his "old brother" when he did dare. "I was really relieved when I heard you had decided to take the plunge!" He guessed his financial troubles and at once bought him a few valuable paintings.

In the autumn of 1938, Blandine finally agreed to a divorce by mutual consent. The proceedings had been initiated. De Prévaux's lawyer followed the case and thought that it would be concluded very soon, especially as Jacques had accepted almost all the terms his wife had demanded: yes, she could keep her married name, yes, he would leave her the furniture. . . . He had nothing but contempt for "the meanness of spirit" of that circle and refused to argue over silver spoons. He would soon be free—broke, but what did that matter? In fact, after the conciliation court hearings, which turned into bitter confrontations, things were to drag on and on. The divorce did not come through until July 1939, on the eve of the outbreak of war.

When he was notified of it, de Prévaux was in Dakar.

11

ON THE *DUGUAY-TROUIN*

Toulon, August 12, 1938. De Prévaux was boarding the cruiser *Duguay-Trouin,* whose command he had just been given. As he walked up the gangway and then inspected the sailors lined up at attention, he thought back to another *Duguay-Trouin,* the training ship on which as a young midshipman just out of the Naval College he had gone on his voyage around the world. Did he imagine at that time that thirty years later it would be he who would be the "old man" directing operations? At twenty, one is so easily dazzled. One dreams of a career pursued at full tilt, of lightning promotions. He hadn't imagined he would have to wait so long.

The 8,000-ton *Duguay-Trouin* cruiser that Jacques now commanded was a modern, extremely seaworthy vessel. Without really overworking her eight boilers, she could reach the remarkable speed of 30 knots. Her dimensions—181 meters long, 17 meters wide—enabled her to carry a significant load of heavy artillery. The crew consisted of nearly six hundred men, twenty-six of whom were officers. For the next ten months, the *Duguay-Trouin* was to form part of the training division of the Mediterranean fleet, and she went to sea only for short coastal trips between Toulon and the Îles de Lérins for firing practice and exercises, interspersed with overhauls and trials.

This ship was a world unto itself. To command a vessel of this size at sea was no sinecure, especially for Jacques, who had little experience of navigation. Until then he had only commanded a gunboat and a sloop. Moreover, owing to bad weather, in the first three days he had to face all the difficulties that usually take a commander six months to master. The officers on the *Duguay-Trouin* had had great respect for their previous commander and doubted the competence of his successor, who had spent almost all his career ashore. They hoped that de Prévaux would be an acceptable commander, but certainly did not expect him to be an "old hand." Naturally, Jacques took up the challenge. He was proud when he made a success of delicate maneuvers, or when he demonstrated his audacity. For instance, during firing practice off Les Salins d'Hyères, in abominable rain with a swelling sea, and a strengthening wind, he decided to carry on. "I held out. All my officers were waiting to see what I would do, and hoping I would give the order to return to anchorage immediately. I kept them in suspense, firing for another hour, to consolidate my authority. It's a hard and rapid apprenticeship, but I believe they already see me as an 'old hand,' which is an achievement."

A week after he had assumed command—"a very splendid and very moving ceremony, the inspection of my whole crew on the immaculate bridge, all those very clean sailors who look you so candidly straight in the eyes, and already with such devotion"—de Prévaux felt at ease onboard. He had moved into the commander's luxurious red and black cabin suite, unpacked his trunks and taken out stacks of books, a few Chinese curios and portraits of Lotka, with which he managed to soften the solemnity of the Empire furniture. Once again he began to do what all seamen do at sea: to sniff the air, to talk about the weather. He worked like a maniac, read Rilke and Péguy in the evenings, and studied foreign political journals at mealtimes in an effort to understand the Czech crisis. He already had his officers well in hand, simply because of his charisma. He liked his ship, he liked his crew, and, as his divorce was now going ahead, Lotka would soon be his wife.

During this time, Europe was marching to Hitler's tune, breathing again each time he pretended to agree to peace. His annexation of Austria in March 1938 didn't cause much excitement in France, which was more concerned with her changes of government and her social problems. Tension rose a little in September at the time of the Sudetenland crisis. Lotka, panic-stricken by the violence of Hitler's speeches at the Nuremberg rally, was certain that war was imminent and wanted to evacuate her parents from Paris. Jacques tried to reassure her: it was only a bluff. Hitler wouldn't go against the advice of his generals and admirals and risk a war that would be lost in advance. And anyway, the diplomats were at work. Paris and London would get Prague to yield once again, if necessary, and would do everything to avoid war even if Hitler invaded Czechoslovakia.... This view was completely impregnated with the "Munich spirit" that dominated French and British foreign policy. Not long afterwards, the success of the Munich Conference reassured public opinion about Germany's intentions. The ogre's appetite seemed to have been appeased; perhaps the firm stand apparently taken by Édouard Daladier, who had succeeded Léon Blum as prime minister, had been effective?

It wasn't until the Prague coup of March 1939, when German tanks invaded Czechoslovakia, that the specter of war once more surfaced, and this time more menacingly. The *Duguay-Trouin* was then undergoing a complete overhaul in Toulon, for one of those periods of repairs and modifications that immobilize a ship for several months. In June, as part of a reorganization of naval forces, the Fifth Squadron was set up and based in Lorient. The *Duguay-Trouin* was part of it and went back to Brittany; the intention was that she should again serve as a training ship. But in the course of the following two months the threats to peace increased. The next target after Czechoslova-

kia was Poland, and the final diplomatic negotiations seemed
less and less likely to prevent the outbreak of hostilities. On August 25, the Fifth Squadron was assembled in Brest. There, the
Duguay-Trouin took its complement of twenty-four torpedoes
onboard and replaced its apprentice gunners with a combat
crew. On the 30th, de Prévaux received onboard Rear Admiral
Moreau, who was to command the squadron, and set sail for
Dakar. By the time he had dropped anchor there, Germany had
invaded Poland, and France and Britain had entered the war.

Lotka hadn't wanted to be present when the cruiser sailed. In
any case, Jacques had been called back from Carnac, where he
had gone to meet her after his shift. She hardly saw him, and his
mind was obviously elsewhere—she might as well go back to
Paris. She detested departures, trains, saying good-bye in harbors, wars, the navy, and ships that cast off their moorings and
took her beloved Jacques away from her. . . . Once again he had
left her, and like so many other times, she was prostrate. What
was going to become of her now, alone in Paris? The beauty
parlor where she had found work had been taken over by an
American company and all the personnel dismissed. For the
last six months she had been trying unsuccessfully to find another job and had been gloomily hanging around at home waiting for her private clients to return. But beauty treatment was
not uppermost in people's minds at that time. She had no
money and, to economize on rent, she lived in the rue Legendre
with her parents. At least she could talk to them about her
beloved. Otherwise, she shut herself away and read, not without
difficulty but conscientiously, *The History of the German Army*
and *The Life of Jesus*. She saw no one now—Jacques was so
jealous, and anyway she never felt like going out. She lived in
expectation of his daily letters, and covered page after page
with her large, elegant writing.

She still couldn't get used to these separations. Every parting was a new wrench and left her feeling more dead than alive. Her love for him was immoderate, absolute; she suffered passionate outbursts, making crazy, anguished vows and resolutions that they must die together. Day after day she cried out to him that she was his slave, that she wanted everything, that she loved him more and more, but that this was still nothing, he would see when they were together again. . . . But for pity's sake, he must write every day or she would die, and he must make his admiral give him leave, because the plain fact was, she couldn't live without him.

But this time their separation, although still as painful, was less tragic. In the first place, Lotka was gradually becoming a sailor's wife. She was becoming like those resigned grass widows, who sniffed the air for the return of their man. She worried about the weather, trembled when she read in *Paris-Soir* that there was a storm in the Mediterranean and that the fleet had had to suspend its exercises and take shelter in Ajaccio. She had been so frightened—"not because of your navigation, good God no, I know you're admirable, but because of that boat, which isn't very reliable." She shivered when she read his impassioned description of the thirty hours he had spent confronting the fury of the elements. She tenderly admonished him: "My love, you've been at sea again. But you know I don't like that at all. I like it when you stay ashore quietly. Don't do it again." Gradually, the questions in her letters about the state of the sea began to merge with those asking "Do you love me forever?"

The divorce had finally been granted. She was reassured of Jacques' love—if it is possible for such a mad passion ever to be sufficiently reassured—and of their life together "for the next forty years." Ever since the proceedings had begun in November 1938, she had expected to be able to marry Jacques the following spring. She had introduced him to her parents. With deep feeling, he had solemnly asked them for the hand of their daughter: "I have become a member of your family," he told her. Bertha and Isidore had succumbed to his charm, and were beside themselves with gratitude for the happiness he was giving their Lotcienka. He had a wealth of filial affection for them, which had been repressed since his mother's death and which he now dared to express. But the divorce case lingered on, and the decree absolute was not pronounced until July 1939, just a few days before the judicial recess.

They still had to wait to marry, and in particular for the official notification of the divorce. After that Jacques had to obtain the navy's permission to remarry. But now he was free. "When we are married," Lotka wrote, "I shall follow you everywhere, and anyway it will be my most absolute right, and even my duty. You will never escape me again, I shan't leave you for a second, even if there's a war. I shall go aboard your ship disguised as a sailor (trousers suit me very well), I shall be your manservant and I shall share your bed. And sometimes they'll hear cries coming from your apartment, and they'll take you for what you aren't. There will be complaints to high places, but since you're a genius and the navy can't do without you, they'll shut their eyes and ears and I shall be able to go on shrieking to my heart's content."

In Dakar, the *Duguay-Trouin* joined the *Primauguet,* another cruiser in the same category. For a month they constituted the Sixth Cruiser Division in the Fifth Squadron, and their mission was to escort French vessels, to cover English convoys on the move, and to patrol on the lookout for enemy craft. Their hunting ground was vast: its northern limit was the Canary Islands, it went down to Sierra Leone, and stretched westwards as far as the thirtieth meridian, roughly the middle of the Atlantic. They sought to intercept German cargo boats that had taken refuge in Africa and were trying to return to their ports, such as the *Amasis* and the *Chemnitz* (the latter was captured). Sometimes they stalked bigger game: the Lufthansa (civil) aircraft carrier *Ostmark,* the auxiliary cruiser *Altmark,* and even the swift, legendary battle cruiser the *Graf Spee.* These interception missions were not always successful. Even when all possible means were deployed, German ships managed to slip through their net. To find a boat that knows it is being hunted and is somewhere between Brazil and the west coast of Africa is looking for a needle in a haystack. This was how the German steamer *Windhuk* managed to escape a combined Franco-British operation, even though the French contributed three cruisers and two destroyers, and the British an aircraft carrier.

De Prévaux was living on the bridge, in the moist, clammy atmosphere of the equatorial zones. He could lie down on a narrow bunk in his chart room, but the commander must always remain on the alert, ready to join his officers of the watch instantly at the slightest alarm. These exhausting voyages of nights on watch and nervous tension, and also often of frustration, alternated with periods of so-called "rest" in port, but there the ship had to be overhauled and submitted to the rigorous inspections, and reports on the patrol written. The rainy season enveloped Senegal in a hot vapor, and sleep became almost impossible in the stifling cabins of the steel boat, where the temperature rose to 35°C with the portholes closed because of the mosquitoes. Another irritation was the presence of the rear admiral on board. While de Prévaux was still the commander of the *Duguay-Trouin,* Admiral Moreau was commander of the whole squadron, and even though their relationship was precisely defined, this was still a difficult situation. De Prévaux felt he had lost some of his independence. For instance, he had to put up with the chore of having his meals with the admiral, and always to be at his disposal. But in the middle of November the Fifth Squadron broke up, and this solved the problem.

Jacques was glad to be able to resume his habit of working on his own once he was off duty. He started reading serious

books again, he began a new diary, he kept up a literary correspondence with several friends, who admired him for still want-
ing to write to them while burdened with all the concerns of the
commander of a cruiser at war. Having become friendly with
Lieutenant Commander Debat, he often asked him into his red
and black cabin, or joined him in the chart room or on the
bridge, cigarette in hand, and during the watches they had eru-
dite conversations about Buddhism or encyclicals, and also discussed politics. Jacques thought highly of this brilliant officer,
and appreciated his culture and his good nature. Georges Debat was at first intimidated by de Prévaux's distant, almost
haughty manner, but he then realized that it was due to
Jacques' fear of intimacy and of being misunderstood. A fear
that was no doubt well-founded, as he tended to express himself in a dense and somewhat esoteric language. And in fact the
crew—respectfully—saw him as "a walking encyclopedia," or
an "egghead."

However, his officers tried to entertain him and get him to go
out with them. Having a car at his disposal, he could move
around a bit, go to the beach, for instance, or to the European
Club. There they danced languorous tangos in the darkness required by the curfew, and they could also amuse themselves in
the bordello. There were several in Dakar, whose charges varied according to what their clients could afford. Chez Maman
Cernay was the most stylish and the most expensive. It was
right in the middle of the town, and the bar, as well as the bun-
galows where the rooms were, opened onto a garden that was a
paradise of flowers and coconut trees. This was the most pleasant place in all Dakar, and the most airy—much more so than
the club. When she heard that the commander of the *Duguay-
Trouin* was coming to see her, Maman Cernay, like a good busi-
nesswoman, came to greet him, and they fell into each other's
arms. They had known each other in Shanghai, earlier in their
respective careers. Since then, they had both been promoted.

De Prévaux generously invited his officers *chez* Maman Cernay, and the sublieutenants trailing in their wake were also granted her favors. It was thanks to Jacques that one young midshipman was allowed to enter this establishment, whose tariffs were far beyond his means, and he remembered this with gratitude. "They treated us like kings, and when we left Dakar the deputy madam gave me a medallion of the Virgin to bring me luck."

On the *Duguay-Trouin* as on the *Altaïr,* Jacques once again immersed himself in thinking about his religious beliefs. He brought out the old volumes of Hindu philosophy from the bottom of his trunk, and the sacred texts that he almost knew by heart: some of the *Upanishads* and the *Bhagavad-Gita,* and Rabindranath Tagore's books. He read everything he could find on Christian spirituality and gave free rein to his religious longings. He didn't actually practice any religion, that was the last thing he wanted, and he refused to call himself a Catholic; he had suffered too much from the "forced, hothouse" religious education imposed on him by the Jesuits. But he had kept Catholicism's faith in a supreme being, a benevolent God, its belief in the individual destiny of man, and a few rites that expressed this confidence: prayer and the cult of the Virgin Mary.

His religious inclinations were now concentrated on the need to believe in the superiority of the forces of the spirit over those of evil, embodied by Hitler. It was more than ever necessary to defend everything that combated Nazi barbarity: Judeo-Christian values. He was convinced that the absolute love that bound him to Lotka was an expression of those values. It had transformed Lotka from a frivolous girl into someone profoundly religious but, in the way of the Slavs, naïvely sentimental, weepy and effusive. Jacques had given her a photo of his mother, who had died when he was a child. "Every evening," she wrote, "I pray to God to send us a miracle to stop this war.

I kiss your dear mother's image and my tears fall on it as I beg her to bless you and watch over you."

What God was she praying to? The Leitners' children, exiled from Poland and cut off from the source of their religion, had almost all lost touch with Judaism, although they didn't abjure it. Lotka had almost forgotten that she was Jewish. The arrival of her parents and the Nazi persecutions had plunged her back into her origins, while her communion of thought and feeling with Jacques encouraged her to express her faith. In September that year she celebrated Yom Kippur with her family. In October, in a fit of anxiety, she made a vow to convert to Christianity if Jacques came back to her safe and sound, and surprised herself by making the sign of the cross and lighting candles in churches. Treachery, no doubt, but it gave her no feelings of remorse.

The *Duguay-Trouin*'s constant patrols had tested her endurance to the limit, but now the ship had to go back to base for overhauls and repairs. As soon as the cruiser that had come to replace her reached the coast of French West Africa, de Prévaux gave the order to set sail on a northward course. It was a difficult crossing, because of the fog and the cold, which the crew had forgotten, and the cross swell, which the vessel didn't like. Finally, on January 18, 1940, she reached Lorient and berthed at the naval dockyard, where she was to be laid up for four months.

No sooner had his leave been granted than Jacques rushed to join Lotka in Paris. She had rented a little flat for them in the block where she had lived before the war, in rue de la Pompe. Ever since she had known he was coming back to her, Lotka had been over the moon. She immersed herself with great relish in the business of moving in and the preparations for their marriage. However hard up they were she must at least have a ring and a dress. . . . Luckily, she still had a whole network of woman friends in couture circles who were more than willing to help her out.

But time was pressing. Jacques' leave would soon be over and the necessary formalities had still not been completed. The official notification of the divorce had finally come through, but the navy made its own demands: Jacques needed its permission for him to marry. To obtain, it he had to provide a personal recommendation signed by his superior officer with reference to "the moral character of his future wife and the suitability of the proposed union." This recommendation was forthcoming after a double inquiry, both civil and military, into "the situation and reputation of the future bride, as well as those of her parents." The police came and interviewed the concierge in rue de la Pompe, and also the one in rue Legendre, where her parents lived. They were sounded out about the people Lotka frequented, her habits, what time she came home at night, alone or not, whether she sometimes stayed out all night. Lotka herself was summoned, and had to submit to close questioning about her parents and her brothers and sisters. The result was satisfactory to the navy, and finally, on February 29, Admiral Devin announced that he "approved this union, which satisfied the moral conditions demanded by the regulations."

Jacques and Lotka were married on March 12, 1940, two days before the end of his Paris leave. But this time they were not parted; she followed him to Lorient. His legitimate wife had the right to appear by his side. They rented a flat in rue du Port, in one of the light, windswept streets surrounding the harbor, just a few minutes away from the dockyard. The spectacular beauty of the commander's young wife created a sensation in this little port. Although she was very discreet, dressed in gray or navy blue, did her best to curb her exuberant temperament, and showed great respect for all the customs and rules of behavior among the officers, nothing could extinguish the radiance of this tall, blonde young woman in the bloom of her thirties.

After six weeks of life together, though, Jacques once again had to concentrate on his command. The *Duguay-Trouin* had been overhauled and repaired, her stability had been improved, her antiaircraft guns reinforced, and she was now ready to put to sea. She was from then on assigned to the French squadron in the eastern Mediterranean, more generally known as Force X. In fact, the *Duguay-Trouin* actually needed a few more days of exercises before going to sea, but the German offensive in the west and the invasion of Belgium and the Netherlands made it necessary to hasten the new squadron's departure to the Middle East. De Prévaux's last days ashore were difficult. He had to get the crew to speed up the indispensable trials, and at the same time do his best to persuade the admiral to allow them a few more days' grace to make sure that the vessel was really operational.

The *Duguay-Trouin* finally set sail on May 17, heading for Alexandria. In spite of the fatigue of the preparations and the pain of having to leave Lotka, de Prévaux relished this departure. He knew that the three months remaining to him to complete his two years of command were the last in his life as a naval officer. He now had no more than a hundred days to enjoy the profound satisfaction of being a commander on the bridge. He could no doubt have left the ship—he would have been found a post on shore, he could have had the happiness of living with Lotka. But his sense of duty was the stronger. He had to complete the normal period of duty of a commander. He owed it to his officers, to his crew, to himself. He expected to be back in mid-August.

12

FORCE X IN ALEXANDRIA

The *Duguay-Trouin* arrived in Alexandria on May 24. The crossing had been trouble free, apart from an alert on leaving Lorient caused by a German submarine cruising nearby. At all events, the crew were permanently at battle stations; one watch prepared for action while the other maintained the equipment and, in whatever time remained, rested. This was an exacting regime and the commander kept them to it with all the necessary rigor, in order to get his six-hundred-odd men to work together with the cohesion indispensable to the battles they all expected to fight.

Force X, under the orders of Vice Admiral Godfroy, was composed of a battleship, four cruisers and three torpedo boats. The purpose of this small, rapid, light and well-armed fleet was on the one hand to preserve free movement along the Suez Canal—a vital route for the Allies—and on the other hand to keep up the pressure on the coasts of Italy if, as seemed probable, Mussolini brought his country into the war. This he did on June 10, 1940, to the great relief of all the sailors, who were spoiling for a fight and certain of defeating the Italian ships. De Prévaux observed that it had been hard for the crew to bear the inaction and the waiting, but "Today we ourselves are going into active service. None of us doubts our victory, or that this victory will be commensurate with the causes we are defending and the sacrifices they will have cost us. And

I know that everyone on board is prepared to make these sacrifices."

But there was to be no naval battle. Although the fleet cruised between the islands, scoured the seas, attempted a raid on the Dodecanese Islands and a landing on Rhodes, then went to Tobruk, in Libya, where an air-reconnaissance patrol thought it had seen some Italian cruisers, the enemy held back and the *Duguay-Trouin* returned to port without having had a chance to fight. The men were so bitterly disappointed that none of them was any longer capable of appreciating the beauty of the Mediterranean shores, where the smooth surface of the sea was gently sparkling in the light.

One last time, on June 22, the squadron was preparing to get under way under the leadership of the British naval forces, also based in Alexandria. It was to take part in a large-scale raid in the Gulf of Taranto, headed by the British fleet under the command of General Sir Andrew Cunningham. This is how de Prévaux explained the operation to his officers: "We know that Italian sailors don't like to leave the shelter of their harbors and minefields. Will they show more courage tomorrow and the day after tomorrow than they did yesterday? Will they still refuse us the action we are longing for? If they do, the four groups of the fleet will conduct independent actions right up to the enemy's coasts. The first three will advance to the Strait of Messina and bombard the large naval base of Augusta, in Sicily. Our group will carry out a raid along the Tripolitanian coast until we are in the vicinity of Tunisia."

There followed exhortations aimed at mobilizing the energies that had been dampened by the alarming news from the front, the order for a general retreat and the occupation of Paris by German troops. "We are all hoping for a fight. . . . Moreover, in these tragic moments for our country, we feel an instinctive need to show ourselves worthy of our brothers in Dunkirk and in the battle of France, to prove to them by our victory over this last-minute enemy the reasons for our unwavering belief in the destiny of France." Furthermore, a victory would call a halt to the growing defeatism in the government. The fleet wanted to fight.

Too late. The order to clear the decks for action was given at 22.30 on June 22. The French ships had already let go their moorings and were on the point of sailing when a first telegram arrived: sailing deferred, followed a few minutes later by a second: sailing canceled. But the British had put to sea, and the crew were at a complete loss. "When I went into the wardroom," Georges Debat related, "all my shipmates, about thirty officers, were clustered around the radio, most of them standing tense and grim-visaged. A senile voice announced the armistice, spoke of honor and dignity, that sort of thing. . . . Then there was silence. Just one or two officers commented:"Since the Marshal [Pétain] says so . . ." But everyone was sad, withdrawn. . . . Very few of them, I know, slept that night."

Onboard the *Duguay-Trouin* there was total consternation. De Prévaux spoke of "treachery," and called on his officers to "grit their teeth and get ready for revenge"—a revenge whose hour was near, they were all convinced. The telegrams and messages, which had succeeded one another since the first indications of negotiations between the belligerents, had at first given rise to a determination to fight on, but then came the humiliation of defeat, and finally the stupefaction at the orders received: they were to surrender before they had even fought, and to hand over their arms intact to yesterday's enemy.

According to the armistice, signed at Rethondes on that very day, June 22, 1940, the undefeated seagoing fleet was not, like the rest of France's military potential, to be handed over to Germany, but was to return to its home bases and there be demobilized and disarmed under the supervision of the victors. This was the condition formulated by the French government, and Hitler had accepted it. In calling on the navy to stop fighting, Darlan, the Admiral of the Fleet, explained this preferential treatment as being "a tribute to the conduct [of the navy] during hostilities and the recognition of its qualities." Darlan swore that he had studied the documents carefully: the clauses of the armistice did not "dishonor" the fleet: it would not be "handed over," but "disarmed under the supervision of Germany." Nuance. He believed Hitler when he gave his word that he would respect our fleet, and found it plausible that the German soldiers would keep a kindly eye on our warships at anchor in occupied Brest, but would not use them. He covered himself by also giving secret orders for sabotage if the enemy or any other foreign forces tried to get hold of French ships.

The navy was thrown into a state of utter confusion. On June 23, Vice Admiral Godfroy called on Force X to be patient and keep calm. He himself didn't yet know the conditions of the armistice but, he stressed, "we are not unaware of what German promises are worth." Three days later, on the 26th, they received the message from Darlan asking them to implement the signed agreements "loyally." How could they not be disconcerted, particularly in the position the French ships now found themselves?

Most of them had been able to leave the Channel and Atlantic ports. Apart from the few that had reached English ports, they had withdrawn to French West Africa or to the Mediterranean, to the two bases of Mers el-Kébir and Alexandria. There they lay at anchor with their former allies who, for their part, were fighting on. Embittered by their enforced inactivity in port, the French seamen cast envious eyes on the English squadrons as they sailed. The English anxiously observed these unscathed ships, immobilized by the armistice agreement, a tempting prey for the enemy and a crucial factor in the continuation of the war if they fell into German hands.

For his part, Churchill did not have Darlan's confidence in Hitler's signature; he was expecting the Germans and Italians, in spite of their promises, to seize the ships that had returned to their French ports. He therefore decided either to win over or neutralize the French fleet, if necessary by force, before it was captured by the enemy and used against the UK. On July 3, Admiral Sir James Somerville, the commander of Force H in Gibraltar, issued an ultimatum to Admiral Gensoul, the commander of the Atlantic forces sheltering in Mers el-Kébir: he was requested to join the British fleet in order to continue the fight, or else to allow his vessels in Mers el-Kébir to be disarmed under British supervision. A further possibility, compatible with honor, was nevertheless offered him: to take his squadron to the West Indies, where it would be neutralized under American supervision. Admiral Gensoul curtly refused, without even discussing them, all the British Admiralty's conditions. The British opened fire, sank the *Bretagne,* and put three other ships out of action. Some thirteen hundred French sailors died in this battle.

The situation in Alexandria was different. In theory, Force X should have gone to Beirut to be disarmed, but it was "detained" in Alexandria. It was not possible for it to sail without the consent of the British: the French fleet was moored at the innermost part of the harbor and in a way trapped; it was a question of *force majeure.* "The British Admiralty, anxious to avoid any risk of our ships falling into the hands of the Germans or Italians if, as had happened so often before, they did not keep their promises, has courteously declared that it finds it necessary to keep us immobilized in Alexandria," Vice Admiral Godfroy announced on June 25. The "courteously" was not pure form. The relations between the two admirals were excellent. Perhaps because Sir Andrew Cunningham was married to a Frenchwoman and Vice Admiral Godfroy's wife was English. The commander of Force X did his best to persuade his officers of the goodwill of the British, and that their recent allies remained their friends.

The tendency in the wardrooms, however, was to distrust the

British, even to hate them. Rather than being a resurgence of the old rivalry between the two fleets, this Anglophobia, carefully fanned by propaganda from the pro-German government established in Vichy, had more to do with recent events. At Dunkirk, had not the British been concerned to evacuate only their own forces, leaving the French soldiers to the mercies of Guderian's armies? Had not London given asylum to a certain de Gaulle, about whom the French radio and press didn't have a good word to say? British suspicions, in short, were considered insulting: as if the French Navy were traitors who would hand over their boats to the Germans or Italians! The friendly feelings between the two admirals, then, were far from being shared by the French crews.

On July 4, the situation very nearly got out of control when notice came of the British ultimatum either to join them or to disarm, which was followed by news of the attack on the fleet at Mers el-Kébir. When the morning watch got up to the quarter-deck they were astounded to see the cruiser *Duguay-Trouin* encircled by British ships anchored fifty meters away, guns leveled on all sides, men at battle stations. A clash seemed inevitable, unless the two admirals, who were in negotiations and whose motorboats were shuttling to and fro, could come up with a solution compatible with both French honor and British security.

It was essential for de Prévaux to do everything possible to avoid a new and absurd bloodbath. He decided to show the British sailors pointing their weapons at the *Duguay-Trouin* that the French Navy—Force X, in any case—had not changed its attitude toward its former allies and in no way saw them as enemies. "Hands to paint ship!" he ordered. They lowered the bosun's chairs and the sailors, suspended in midair a few dozen meters away from the mouths of the British guns, started scrubbing enthusiastically, whistling nonchalantly. The officers watched the Englishmen's embarrassment with amusement: wasn't there something a little ridiculous about holding a group

of men in your sights while they were peacefully painting their
hull? Could the British Admiralty really give the order to fire
on an unarmed crew busily going about their daily chores?

Suddenly there was the sound of a bombardment. But it
wasn't the English firing on the French. It was an Italian air
raid. The British fleet responded, naturally. So did Force X—
spontaneously, without waiting for orders, which would probably not have been given. At the end of the alert both crews
returned to their posts, the English once again pointing their
guns at the French, and the French going back to their buckets
of paint. But the tension had gone down a notch.

This situation couldn't last. The two admirals disapproved of
the ultimatum Churchill had ordered, whose consequences
could only be absurd: shedding French and British blood for
the benefit of the enemy. Nevertheless it needed a great deal of
goodwill on both sides to get over the disastrous effects of the
Mers el-Kébir attack. After a few hours they came to a gentle-
man's agreement. Sir Andrew Cunningham undertook not to
try to seize the French ships by force, in exchange for Admiral
Godfroy's word that his fleet wouldn't try to sail and would not
scuttle its ships. The crew of Force X would remain free and
could go ashore; only the reservists would be demobilized. This
agreement remained in force until 1943.

"At first we made every endeavor to resist," de Prévaux wrote.
Just before the armistice there had been some hope of continuing the fight from the Middle East. General Mittelhauser, who
had replaced Weygand as commander in chief in Syria, had declared that he was against the armistice and was ready to continue the struggle alongside the British. But he soon had to bow
to the orders of Weygand and Darlan, and to Darlan's assurances that the fleet would remain intact. His submission, like
that of General Noguès in Rabat, was to become a determining
factor in the choice offered to Force X: either to implement the

armistice agreement "loyally," that's to say remain idle in harbor in Alexandria, or to join the movement de Gaulle was starting in London, the Free French Naval Forces.

The general's appeal was probably not heard onboard the *Duguay-Trouin,* but the news reached the men shortly afterwards through the sailors' contacts on shore. Their reaction was more than mixed. At first, they had confidence that the liberal-minded Vice Admiral Godfroy would be able to find a solution compatible with the honor of the navy. Then they began to believe the assurances of Darlan—the Admiral of the Fleet!—and, of course, of Pétain—the Marshal, the conqueror of Verdun! And finally, Vichy propaganda and indignation at the Mers el-Kébir massacre turned the crews against the idea of fighting with the British. What was more, it so happened that the men who had met the Alexandrian Gaullists ashore didn't get along with them. Some because "they had got themselves comfortably established in Egypt with their businesses while they sent everyone else off to fight"; others because they were rich oriental Jews, whose "tactless enthusiasm" for Gaullism had reawakened the anti-Semitism latent in the fleet. As for the sailors who had joined de Gaulle, they were regarded as "dubious."

All these arguments helped to reinforce the tendency of the navy, a politically conservative organization, to accept an authority that claimed to represent the moral order and the immutable values of Christian France. It couldn't be otherwise, Georges Debat observed, "in a navy in which all the officers' wardrooms had received *L'Action française** every day for twenty years." So there is nothing astonishing about the fact that only an infinitesimal number of sailors joined de Gaulle in 1940: among the Force X crews immobilized in Alexandria there were fewer than two hundred.

*L'Action française was an extreme right-wing newspaper propagating the Catholic monarchist and anti-Semitic views of a political group of the same name.

* * *

Lieutenant Commander Honoré d'Estienne d'Orves was a member of the first group that left for London on July 9. Before he left, he wanted to talk to de Prévaux, whose spirit of resistance and sympathy with de Gaulle was well known. D'Orves knew that although de Prévaux had been trained like every other naval officer to an almost automatic obedience to orders passed down through the chain of command, his spirit would not allow him to consent to defeat. For him, armistice or no armistice, "our enemies have never ceased to be the Germans." Not the proud people he had come to esteem in Berlin, but a totalitarian, criminal and racist system. In the long conversations de Prévaux had with Debat, he stigmatized this "collapse of all the values that constituted our pride and dignity." To confront the Nazi regime was not a question of "a simple Franco-German war . . . but of a fight to the death of the spirit against the religion of race and blood." Moreover, whereas the majority of officers could recognize themselves in the France personified by Marshal Pétain, de Prévaux deplored not only the French military defeat, but also France's failure to face up to its responsibilities, its too readily accepted surrender, and the allegiance of a whole people to the person of its leader.

In that case, should he join the movement organized in London by de Gaulle? Jacques thought highly of him. He had studied his theories on tank warfare and approved of his innovatory ideas on tactics. If the army had followed the recommendations of the young Colonel de Gaulle and agreed to modify its defense policy, Guderian's tanks would have found themselves confronted by solid armored divisions. And finally, de Prévaux admired the sense of honor and the courage of this officer who had refused to obey orders.

After his talk with d'Estienne d'Orves, Jacques nevertheless decided to stay aboard the *Duguay-Trouin.* As he explained to Debat, it was a question of responsibility. Lieutenant Commander d'Estienne d'Orves was Admiral Godfroy's aide-de-camp; he was a junior officer whose job was about to be reduced to almost nothing; his departure for London would be of no great consequence to Force X; and finally, his decision affected no one but himself. The situation of the commander of the *Duguay-Trouin* was very different, since he was responsible for the ship and the crew, and it was important that they should remain operational while waiting for the moment when the situation would be reversed and the interrupted combat could finally be resumed, when Jacques was convinced that France would regain her honor. He was not free to make a personal decision. Once he was relieved of his command, though, he wouldn't hesitate to commit himself.

This reasoning, which was that of many naval officers who sincerely supported the Free French, explains why so few of them joined de Gaulle in that summer of 1940. Only one flag officer, Vice Admiral Muselier, forced to retire by Darlan, reached London, where he met the general without actually knowing what he was getting into, and of the seventy-two sailors from Force X who joined the Free French, there were only nine officers, the most senior being Commander Auboyneau, whose rank was just below that of de Prévaux.

In August, Jacques fell ill—his anemia had returned—recovered, had a relapse, and finally had to be sent back to France.

His farewells on the *Duguay-Trouin* were very moving. It was his last ship, his last seagoing command, and the crew gathered together to salute the colors one last time. The day before he left, the petty officers invited him to a farewell drink. Crowded together in their quarters, which were not designed to hold so many men at once, they spoke awkwardly of their loyalty, their blind confidence in him, their duty, and the wonderful memories of their commander that would always remain with them. "We have a sincere affection for you, Commander." Se-

PART III

VOX AND KALO

13
IN THE MARITIME COURT

De Prévaux landed in Toulon in November 1940. To his great surprise, Lotka was there waiting for him.

Ever since her husband had sailed on May 17, she had been distraught, as she always was when they were separated. It had been worse this time, as she didn't know where he was, since Jacques was not allowed to say where Force X was going. She had guessed, though, that he was in the eastern Mediterranean and deduced, from a few allusions to "a country whose mythology is so complicated," that it must be Egypt. Knowing that the *Duguay-Trouin* was nowhere near the combat zone had reassured her—until Italy entered the war. She had had no news from Jacques during the whole of the five months he had been away. She, as always, had sent him letters and telegrams, not suspecting that they had never reached him.

Added to the distress of separation were her financial worries—she hadn't a sou—and the panic of every air-raid warning; she had promised Jacques to be sensible and go down to shelter in the cellar. She soon realized that it would be a good idea to take their most precious possessions with her—the magnificent porcelain dinner service, the jades, the ivory Chinese virgin, and she exhausted herself going up and down stairs. Every day the din of the bombardment seemed to get nearer to Paris.

She was desperately worried about her parents. Roland de

Margerie had warned her of the speed of the German advance
and advised her to evacuate them within the hour. The day before the Germans entered the capital, she and her parents
joined the stream of Parisians fleeing the Occupation and
found refuge in Lude, a village near Le Mans. But the peace of
the village only increased her anxiety. She imagined that
Jacques' letters had finally arrived and were piling up with the
concierge in the rue de la Pompe. How could she have been
guilty of such dereliction of duty—not being there to read
them? She couldn't stand it any longer and went back to Paris,
but found nothing. She then spent August in Cheilly with her
sister-in-law Jeanne.

When she heard, in mid-October, that Jacques was going to
be repatriated, she immediately decided to go to Toulon. It was
a dangerous undertaking to travel down the whole length of
France, and cross the demarcation line separating the occupied
north from Vichy France, and she would need a permit to enter
the free zone. How was she to get one? A bored official explained the procedure: she simply had to produce a medical certificate proving that her husband was in hospital in Toulon and
that his life was in danger. She should wait until she had it and
then come back and put in her request. Lotka could see how
long all this would take, with the administrative delays and the
uncertainties of the mail. It was out of the question for her to
mope around in Paris when Jacques was ill on French soil. She
didn't hesitate but jumped into a train, telling herself that she
would be perfectly capable of "crossing the line whistling to myself, my hands in my pockets." Somehow she managed it and was
waiting on the dock when the boat bringing Jacques back from
Alexandria came alongside.

He was on sick leave. According to the diagnosis of Force X's
doctor, he was suffering from hemolytic anemia and hyperten-
sive nephritis. His sick leave had surprised his subordinates,

who had no idea of the gravity of his state of health; some of them even envied him for being able to return to France sooner.

Certainly, de Prévaux had found the compulsory inactivity of Force X in Alexandria hard to bear. He was bored and miserable on a ship stuck in port among a somnolent squadron. The moment they were given permission to leave the ship, the crew lived ashore and enjoyed themselves playing tennis at the Sporting Club or livening up the atmosphere at garden parties. The sailors settled down, putting down roots and finding girlfriends. The headmaster of the lycée, Marcel Fort, had put his playing fields at their sailors' disposal but soon turned them out, "exasperated at seeing them playing football as if nothing had happened." Some of the officers rented a flat in the town. As usual, the minor events of society life held no charm for Jacques. In any case he rarely went ashore, preferring to stay onboard in his luxurious cabin reading, writing long letters to Lotka almost daily, or having discussions with Georges Debat.

No matter how bored he was, though, and how much he longed to be with Lotka, it wasn't his style to report sick. Nevertheless, on October 7 the general staff of Force X ordered his repatriation for health reasons, via Jerusalem and Beirut. He was asked to take advantage of his journey to take some diplomatic bags with him. His state was regarded as serious, so he was authorized to travel by sleeper, an exceptional favor. And he was sent to hospital when he arrived in Lebanon, before traveling on the hospital ship *Sphinx* to Toulon. Here, it was intended that once restored to health he should resume his service in the third maritime region.

Jacques was confident of being given a new posting very quickly. Scrupulously conscientious, a tireless worker, he prided himself on never being ill, and spoke condescendingly of people who allowed themselves that luxury. Very shortly after he was back, then, he rushed off to Vichy and tried to see Darlan and get a posting: he was hoping for "a diplomatic post a long way away." He hung around for a while in the antichambers of the ministry, met quite a few people, but got nothing but vague promises and returned to Toulon empty-handed.

Lotka and he were then living in Le Canadel, in an unremarkable house with an ugly name, La Villa Binder. But what did that matter? Seven years after having fallen in love with one another, eight months after their marriage, they were finally beginning their life together. Since all they had had up till then was a mere handful of weeks together, squeezed between Jacques' naval duties and his conjugal obligations, however minimal, setting up house like this had something lasting about it. To call it their life together, however, does not do it justice. Jacques described just what it meant to them both in a letter to Kouba Distenfeld, the husband of Lotka's younger sister Mania: "Lotka and I, after so many months of anguish following so many years of waiting, have at last been permitted to surrender ourselves entirely to this happiness we have finally achieved, which from now on we shall never again allow to escape us." And yet this incredible, unwearying happiness in which they were living "one through the other and one for the other" was again about to be interrupted. Jacques had to watch his health. He was sent to the military hospital in Toulon, where he had to obey doctors' orders and above all submit to the High Commission for Health in the navy, on whose opinion his return to active service depended.

At first he was terribly bored. He missed what he loved best in the world: Lotka and books. Before he went into hospital he had explored the town's bookshops but hadn't been able to find the Gides he wanted to have on his bedside table. He did succeed, however, in getting permission to go out, which in theory was strictly forbidden, even to officers. "But," he frankly admitted, "from the very beginning I got them to understand that I didn't consider their rules were made for me, and they accepted that with good grace."

Between sick leaves and repeated convalescent leaves, his health gradually improved. While his anemia was cured by rest and treatment, his hypertension persisted and justified an extension of his leave. This now delighted de Prévaux, who was overjoyed at the idea of being able to spend another two months with Lotka, especially since they had moved into a charming villa at Pramousquier. In Toulon, Jacques was sickened by "the discouraging atmosphere of flabbiness, acceptance and acclimatization."

After six months, in July 1941, he finally received his assignment, which rather surprised him—but he was sure it would only be temporary, until Vichy found him a "real" posting. He was appointed Chairman of the First Permanent Maritime Court in Toulon, where he was to replace Commander Bonnot. In order for him to master the unfamiliar judicial functions, he was granted one short month of training. At the end of it he proudly observed that he already understood it all, and that even though the other judges were much younger, he was much more capable than they of putting up with the length and aridity of the hearings in overheated rooms, that he could quite happily continue until the evening. He also felt that with him justice might be done in a fashion that was less brutally expeditious and less often negligent.

In his office on the first floor of the port's prefecture (the official residence of the chief of police) in the Place des Armes, studying the enigmatic dossiers which were passed on to him only at the last minute, he enjoyed resuming his old habit of working at night and abandoned himself to his obsession of doing everything thoroughly. Otherwise, he lived the life of a hermit, as he always had since he met Lotka, and went on writing his daily letters to her, full of declarations of love and entreaties "not to flirt with either men or women," and telling her of the terrible wrench it was to have to leave her on Monday mornings until the following Friday. . . .

But Vichy soon realized that de Prévaux was the wrong choice for a job whose purpose was to punish sailors who had rallied to the Free French. His rigor, his independent spirit and his determination to try to convince his opponents made him a very good chairman, but not a pawn. Moreover, his judgments revealed his bias in favor of resistants. During this period the Toulon maritime court had the reputation of being severe with those Frenchmen who supported the occupier and indulgent toward the patriots who had already joined the Resistance. While he was not yet committed to the Resistance movement, de Prévaux had made his choice, and occasionally expressed it.

Besides, he had some extremely suspicious contacts, for instance with Colonel Paillole. The colonel had started an information bureau under the innocuous name of Rural Works and later joined General Giraud's secret service. In 1940–41 he was engaged in counter espionage for the Vichy Bureau of Anti-National Activities; his underground command post was in Marseille. Colonel Paillole testified that "the Toulon naval base was far and away the greatest supporter in the region of the budding Resistance movement, and this was due to the decisive prompting of Jacques de Prévaux."

It was also possible that Vichy's information bureau, whose chief was Darlan, had gotten wind of the suspicious events going on in the maritime prison housed in the arsenal. It was not that prisoners had disappeared, but that packages were appearing in the prison. These contained the most secret archives of the counterespionage services for which, at considerable risk to himself, de Prévaux found this unusual hiding place.

De Prévaux's dismissal came abruptly and without warning. On December 16 he was summoned by Vice Admiral Marquis, the port admiral, who informed him that the headquarters of the third maritime region had "granted" him extended leave. In fact, the order came from Vichy. The document he was given carried the letterhead of the office of the secretary of state for the navy, and the signature, dated the 14th, of Darlan, Admiral of the Fleet and minister of national defense. De Prévaux flinched at the word "granted," and was amazed: he had made no request for leave. He discovered that he was one of the first victims of the law of November 8, 1941 dealing with *congés d'activité* (suspension from active duty) for officers. Its text was unambiguous: "In no case may a *congé d'activité* be granted on demand." It was the result of a "decision" made by the secretary of state (i.e., Darlan), to whom the officer was subordinate. One eccentricity of the administration was that the decree required the port admiral to show the text of the law in question to the parties concerned, but "not to allow them to take a copy of it," and, above all, not to refer to it in the documents. . . . In the past, Admiral Darlan had had occasion to report on de Prévaux. In 1937, as chief of naval staff, he wrote on the service record of the new auditor at the Centre des hautes études navales: "Slovenly appearance"—which was hardly Jacques' style—"intelligent, too much of an intriguer."

The admiral, somewhat embarrassed, gave Jacques the paper to sign, explaining that it came within the overall policy of appointing younger officers, intended to prevent the promotion of all those who were considered too old. This argument wasn't even plausible: at fifty-three, Jacques would have been young for a rear admiral (the average age of active rear admirals in 1941 was fifty-seven), and if the average age had to be brought down at all costs, why didn't they start with the forty-three captains who were older than he, or the hundred or so who had more seniority?

De Prévaux had quite simply been dismissed from his post, after a complaint had been made about his indulgence toward sailors branded as "deserters," and his laxity in carrying out orders from Vichy, which demanded exemplary punishments. In July 1941—before Jacques assumed his responsibilities—

among the sentences pronounced by all the courts martial there were death (in three cases), twenty years' imprisonment, loss of nationality, dishonorable discharge—not to mention the withdrawal of allowances to the families of "dissidents."

That evening, while he was putting his uniforms away for the last time, de Prévaux felt shattered. So, just like that, the navy was over. The métier he loved, the joy of commanding, his studious night watches set against the reassuring background of the calm drone of the machines, the crew lined up in review order, the precise maneuvers, the discipline and the affection, it had all come to an end. Thirty-five years of his life. His pride as a career officer suffered from having been thrown out so brutally. But would he still have been able to hope for promotion, after eight months of waiting for a post in the guise of the chairman of a maritime court?

At dawn, after a sleepless night, de Prévaux saw his situation in a different light. At least, from now on, he could "be himself, with no more shilly-shallying or hypocrisy." Rather than worry himself sick waiting in vain for clear battle orders against the enemy's armies, for instructions to resist the occupier, he was at last free to devote all his strength and all his time to the fight for the liberation of France. It was no longer his duty to refuse to commit himself, he was no longer obliged to obey orders that came down through the chain of command, which had so far always ended by overriding the duty dictated by his conscience.

In any case, just the day before, he had begun to assert his independence. Telling Admiral Marquis exactly what he thought of his discharge, he had declared which side he had chosen: "There is nothing dishonorable, now, in being counted among the proscribed—far from it."

A fine declaration of Gaullist faith. Darlan had no idea that in dismissing de Prévaux he was offering the Resistance a great leader.

14

COMMITMENT

The decisive encounter took place in November 1941. De Prévaux hadn't waited to be "granted leave" by the navy before getting in touch with a Resistance network. And the middle-aged man who unobtrusively entered a Toulon bistro to keep a clandestine rendezvous was taking a great risk; he was the chairman of the maritime court.

He was there to meet one of the local leaders of the F2 network. On that chilly morning, Auguste-Henry Brun (Volta)* pushed open the door of the Café de la Rade in Toulon harbor. It was the hour of the midmorning break, and the café was packed with workers from the arsenal noisily discussing the latest news. No one took any notice of him, and anyway everyone knew him by sight, even though he wasn't a naval man but a militant member of the Christian Socialist Trade Union, CFTC, who often went the rounds of the bistros. Walking past the tables, he replied to several greetings as he looked around the smoke-filled room in search of the unknown "friend" he had come to meet.

"He's about fifty and looks severe," John Ulysse Mentha (Certigny) had told him. "He'll be waiting for you in the back room, by the door. Watch out, he's a bigwig: a Gaullist naval officer who wants to join the Free French."

*Each member of the Resistance had a *nom de guerre,* or code name. This is given in parentheses at the first mention.

"Too good to be true," Brun had muttered. "He's probably been sent to infiltrate us. I'll risk getting my cover blown. And that's the last thing the group needs at this moment. Had you thought of that?"

The little group of resistants Brun belonged to was going through a difficult period. Arrests in the district had been on the increase and they had tightened their security precautions.

"Several of us have seen him and we're sure he's genuine. Here are your instructions: when you've spotted him, you go up and shake his hand. Then he'll say . . ."

But the meeting took place in an unusual way. The "friend" identified Brun first and took the initiative: he got up and went over to him. Was this contempt for elementary precautions due to ignorance of clandestine procedure, or was it a way of getting the upper hand? Bad beginning, thought Brun, furious at the new recruit's imprudence. He didn't hide this bad impression from his chiefs. "I went to the rendezvous and it was Vox who contacted me. He knew perfectly well who I was, and that was unpleasant, for security reasons." Brun was suspicious, and didn't immediately reveal his identity. True, the man had given him the password, but he could still be an agent provocateur, and was that the way an officer would behave? No, the resistant concluded. "And I only showed my hand when he gave me the name of a high-up officer as a reference, the second in command of the *Tourville*.

Two months and several interviews later, Jacques de Prévaux (Vox) became a member of the F2 network. He started working for them officially in April 1942, but in the autumn of 1941 he was already involved in the Resistance.

It was thanks to his few months as chairman of the maritime court that de Prévaux had made indirect contact with the F2 network of the Toulon Resistance in the autumn of 1941.

Jacques had made the acquaintance of a man called Abrahams, either through his sister, a barrister who had been the defending counsel in a case Jacques had tried, or through a mutual friend called Gérard. The two men took to each other, discovered they both admired Péguy, and at Abraham's house in Toulouse Jacques again saw the poet Léon-Paul Fargue, whom he had already met in Paris. Jacques went to see the Abrahams every week—his only outing in Toulon, for what he drolly called "my non-Aryan bridge." Did they really only play cards?

Marcel Abraham had other talents. This brilliant academic, chief inspector of schools in the Paris district, had been Jean Zay's principal private secretary before being relieved of his responsibilities in 1940. Forced to leave Paris after the breakup of the Musée de l'Homme network, he had taken refuge in Toulon, where he had family. He was a member of the Franc Tireur Resistance movement and an occasional contributor to the underground newspaper of the same name.

The origin of this branch of the Resistance, which had been started in Lyon in the autumn of 1940, was the determination of a handful of friends to continue the fight against the occupier. Embittered and enraged, they rejected the armistice and repudiated the Vichy regime. The founding members, wrote D. Veillon, "were left-leaning socialists, radicals, militants of *Jeune République.* While they protested against Hitler and Nazism ... they associated their political aims (re-establishment of republican liberties, return to democracy and nationalization) with the fight against the occupier, and that was one of its original features." Franc Tireur, though, wanted to unite everyone fighting for liberty, or rather for the liberties and rights of man, without class or ideological sectarianism. They were not playing politics, and it was out of the question, for instance, to adopt the anticlerical tone usually to be found in radical circles. These nuances are important in explaining why de Prévaux supported the civic and moral options of Franc Tireur and F2.

At first the group distributed tracts signed "France-Liberté" in Lyon; then, at the instance of Jean-Pierre Lévy, who had become the national leader, it expanded outside Lyon and spread over the whole of unoccupied France. The monthly paper *Franc Tireur* was founded in order to support the movement's activities. When Jean-Pierre Lévy was looking for someone to take charge of the southern zone, a regimental comrade gave him the name of Frank Arnal. Arnal, the son of a gendarme, was a member of the Socialist Party, and a convinced republican. Serving behind the counter of his Pharmacie de la Poissonnière, he knew all Toulon and was also the president of the pharmacists' trade union in the Var. Yet Arnal refused to commit himself to Franc Tireur—because he was already a member of F2—but he gave Lévy the name of John Ulysse Mentha, whose house had been used as the network's first mailing address. At that time, and for a long time afterwards, the various movements and networks were in close contact, and in spite of instructions to be prudent they carried out missions for each other, depending on who had the best opportunity. Mentha accepted the task entrusted to him by Jean-Pierre Lévy and promoted the *Franc Tireur* in the Midi.

So Marcel Abraham told Mentha about his meeting with de Prévaux, whose sympathies lay with de Gaulle, Jacques never having made any secret of this. At a party given by Marcel Abraham in the Place d'Armes in Toulon, de Prévaux had met Jacques Lévy-Rueff, a naval engineer who, under the code name of Vir, was later to become his deputy in the Toulon sector of F2. Lévy-Rueff remembered perfectly what was said in Abraham's mother's drawing room, which was far from innocuous. De Prévaux had expressed his pro-Gaullist sentiments. He may also have let it be known then that he wanted to go to London.

Jacques asked everyone he met the same question: how did one go about rallying to de Gaulle in London? An awkward question. Mentha had no radio and no means of establishing contact. On the other hand, Azur, the F2 group in Toulon, was in regular contact with London. Mentha, who knew not only Frank Arnal but also Auguste-Henry Brun, decided to ask them to check and test this unlikely recruit.

After Brun had made the first contact with de Prévaux in the Café de la Rade, another Christian socialist trade unionist, Gaston Havard (Foch), a higher-ranking member of Azur-F2, met him in a bistro on the Quai de Cronstadt. Foch reported: "He was with his young wife. I questioned him, and then told him that I had no direct means of sending him to England but that I could try to get a message passed on through my network. In the meantime, he put himself at my disposal. I then explained exactly what we did, told him my name and my profession: a clerk at the arsenal. He insisted that he wanted to be under my orders and that he accepted the strict discipline we observed. I started putting him to the test by giving him some simple missions. This ship's captain, who had been through staff college and was a former naval attaché in Berlin, proved himself remarkably obedient to the orders of the simple arsenal worker that I was and submitted with a smile to this situation which, to say the least, was bizarre."

15

F2 — A FRANCO-POLISH NETWORK

June 1940. The armistice had been signed, and the Polish army fighting in France was retreating. Only a handful of the troops managed to find transportation; many were stranded on the Atlantic coast. The last boat had just sailed from Saint-Jean-de-Luz (near Biarritz) in the midst of indescribable chaos, leaving thousands of bewildered soldiers behind. Among them were two Polish officers of a special kind: Major Vincent Zarembski and Major Rygor Slowikowski, former intelligence officers. At first they worked in an organization that arranged clandestine passages for soldiers to Spain. Later they set up an intelligence service in France — a professional reflex, in a way. They had no contact with their headquarters, no radio, at least to begin with, but they started recruiting "pianists," confident that the time would come when they would be able to communicate with the Allies.

At the same time the Polish admiralty, which had taken refuge in London with General Sikorski and the Polish government in exile, decided to create a naval intelligence network in France. They finally found the right person for this difficult mission: Tadeusz Jekiel, a marine engineer. For a time he had been seconded to the French Navy and was familiar with both France and French naval circles, which qualified him to enlist recruits who must necessarily be French. On the other hand, all his knowledge of intelligence came from what he had read in detective stories. He was put through a crash course for a few weeks and then in September sent to Marseille, taking with him a handful of names of possible contacts.

To start with, he joined forces with his compatriot Zarembski, told him of London's agreement and gave him a crystal set and the signaling codes. Vincent Zarembski (Tudor) lived in Marseille until December 1941, when his cover was blown and he had to leave. He later became the head of the Polish intelligence network Ekspozytura-France, which discontinued its activities at the end of 1942. His colleague Rygor Slowikowski left for Algeria in August 1941 and set up the North Africa network.

Once in the Midi, Tadeusz Jekiel (Doctor) made other contacts which led to the formation of the F2 network. He very soon met Léon Sliwinski (Jean-Bol), for whom he had a letter, and who "had an unbelievable talent for making the acquaintance of people who would be useful to the success of his projects," and then Gilbert Foury (Edwin). In the restaurant car of a train, he happened across a colleague he had known in Le Havre: Jacques Lévy-Rueff, the man Jacques had met at Marcel Abraham's. He finally met François Horowicz (François), who, in spite of his Polish name, was actually French. An electrician in a firm that worked for the Toulon dockyard, he had become friendly there with Gaston Havard.

One day Horowicz told Jekiel of the existence of a small group of resistants in Toulon who, with Havard, were examining the possibilities of liaising with the Free French in England. "Since we don't accept the armistice," Havard wrote in his memoirs, "we must act according to our principles and try to carry on the struggle. . . . But how can we act effectively? We consider that actual fighting in France would at the moment be premature. There are only three lines of possible action open to us: propaganda, sabotage, intelligence. . . . But we are well aware that the effect of this work will be practically nonexistent unless we have some contact with the armed forces: London. How can we manage to get in touch with the English?"

In the meantime, Havard went on recruiting and setting up clandestine communication channels. This energetic, authoritarian little man turned out to be an outstanding organizer. Although far from gifted as a horticulturalist, he founded an association of jobbing gardeners in the Var as a cover for meetings and movements. And he never stopped asking all his trusted friends the vital question of how to make contact with London, the same question de Prévaux had been asking himself—to which Jekiel had the answer.

Thanks to François Horowicz, the link between the Toulon resistants and the envoy from London was finally made. One evening in October 1940, Tadeusz Jekiel visited Gaston Havard. They saw that their objective was the same and that the means at their disposal were complementary—Havard had the men, and Jekiel the transmission equipment—and decided to work together. They would concentrate solely on intelligence. In this way the Azur network, the true beginning and nucleus of F2, was established, thanks to the meeting of an officer sent by Polish headquarters in London, an agent from the dockyard, a marine engineer, a pharmacist, a university professor, and an electrician.

F2 started operating in Nice. It developed rapidly under the direction of Jekiel, helped by Sliwinski, and very soon acquired its own means of transmission. Unlike Ekspozytura-France and the Polish resistance movement POWN, it was mainly composed of Frenchmen to whom their Polish leaders taught the practice of covert action, which was more common in Poland than in France. Another difference was that it was to remain active until the Liberation. Finally, its agents, unlike those in the Tudor network, were not intelligence professionals, but resistants whose services were later to be recognized as services in the ranks of France at war. Not mercenaries, but convinced patriots, as their efficiency on the ground was to show the professionals in the London headquarters of the intelligence service, immersed in their dossiers. The information they provided was not paid for, unlike that of the professional agents. The subsidies sent by the Polish General Staff to the F2 network (the money ultimately came from the British secret services) were used to cover their expenses and to help their agents by providing them with ration cards for bread and cigarettes, as well as supporting their families in case of arrest. Finally, these were militants with a single cause: liberation from the Nazi stranglehold. The nationality of the agents, their class, their political or religious opinions, were not of the slightest importance in the struggle against the common enemy.

When de Prévaux was recruited by Havard in November 1941, he had no idea of the Polish component of the network he was entering, since his companions and his direct chief were French. He was most surprised to learn that his chief, Sliwinski, was a compatriot of Lotka. And anyway, more and more Frenchmen were being recruited.

But although the organization was autonomous, F2 had been incorporated into the administration of the Tudor network, which in practice meant that the information it gathered went to the Second Bureau of the Polish General Staff in London. That was all—but it was a great deal. It meant that the organization was run by the Poles, a fact that most of the agents were unaware of, since for obvious security reasons they knew only their immediate contacts and only by their code names. At the Liberation, some of them would be furious to discover that they had in fact worked in a network of "White Poles," and indignant at the opacity—however necessary in an intelligence service—within the hierarchy. This sometimes led to ludicrous situations, such as when two agents' paths crossed at Rose

16

THE SUBTERFUGE

Barely two months after their meeting on Quai de Cronstadt, Havard was already in a position to appreciate the work de Prévaux had accomplished. His contacts with senior naval officers were irreplaceable, and his qualities as an organizer invaluable. The network wanted to keep him, and suggested that he shouldn't go to London but continue working in France.

De Prévaux agreed—on quite unusual conditions. The first was outrageous: he wanted to get to know the leader of the network personally. Given his rank and the services he could render, they decided to make an exception, and granted it. In any case, Sliwinski was reassured by the fact that de Prévaux's wife was Jewish: it would have been dangerous for the couple to betray the Resistance.

The second condition was more delicate. De Prévaux wanted to know for whom, ultimately, he was working. If he gave up—provisionally, he thought—the idea of joining the Free French in London, where his rank would entitle him to a top job, he wanted to have a guarantee that in Toulon he was really working for General de Gaulle. More precisely, he wanted to receive the order to work with F2 directly from the general. The other F2 agents were content to know that the information they gathered reached the Allies, the essential thing for them being to fight the occupier effectively. Paradoxically, while Jean Moulin was actively engaged in getting various Resistance movements to combine, de Prévaux, for his part, was fighting to be officially affiliated to the Gaullist movement. In vain, as we shall see.

This concern for recognition, which never left him, is easy to explain. In the first place, de Prévaux was above all a Gaullist — his friends called him "de Prévaux-the-Gaullist." And he was a loyalist; his education, his military training, his career as an officer, had all taught him obedience and allegiance to legal authority. Once he'd taken the plunge of rebelling against the orders of his own hierarchy, de Gaulle became his source of legitimacy.

Moreover, even though he had been discharged by Darlan, even though he had become a secret agent in a Toulon intelligence network, he still considered himself to be a naval officer. His superiors were now the Free French Naval Forces (FNFL). His career was continuing within their movement. But the particular context (the war, the Vichy regime, his discharge) justified him in demanding that his personal situation vis-à-vis the FNFL be clarified.

De Prévaux, finally, was not a politician. Never having been really interested in movements or political parties or in the balance of power, he barely understood and was suspicious of them. Called upon to join a Resistance group, he was afraid of being manipulated and wanted some guarantee. Fears, that in the end would be justified.

De Prévaux and Sliwinski first met on January 25, 1942. Sliwinski had informed the Polish General Staff in London (telegram F/448/42) of de Prévaux's request, and had been assured that Vox's work in the network would indeed be considered as service in the ranks of the *Forces françaises libres* (FFL). A way still had to be found to give de Prévaux proof that the Free French Forces agreed to his appointment. It was arranged that the BBC's French program would broadcast a phrase of his choice.

At La Cisampo, their little house in the hills above Pramousquier, Jacques and Lotka were waiting for Sliwinski or, more exactly, for Jean-Bol. Lotka had brought out the jade goblets and the last bottle of Noilly Prat and was wondering whether that wasn't too frivolous for this sort of occasion. She didn't dare say a word to Jacques, who was smoking like an automaton and staring at the wall, looking even more serious than usual. The ashes were falling on the floor but he didn't react when she pushed the ashtray toward him. His obstinate silence showed her that his nerves were on edge: Was it the idea of meeting the head of the network, the prospect of receiving material proof of F2's connection with the forces of General de Gaulle? When Jean-Bol arrived, they were somewhat surprised to see that he was a tall and vivacious young man of twenty-six, with a determined look. He kissed Lotka's hand with great elegance.

"Let me suggest a simple way to give you the guarantee that you really are working for de Gaulle," said Jean-Bol. "If you choose a particular phrase and hear it on the radio from London in their 'Les Français parlent aux Français' program, will that convince you?"

"I think so," Jacques replied.

"Then choose one."

Jacques was silent for a few seconds, and then said in a firm voice:

"Right. Here is my message: 'J'embrasse ma Lotka chérie.'"

Jean-Bol wrote this down, then went over to the window and unobtrusively threw the paper over the garden fence. He had stationed Bey, one of his agents, in the street, with orders to pick it up and go immediately to telephone its contents to the exchange in Nice. There, Lubicz, the cryptographer, would transmit it to London, following the network's usual procedures. The whole operation would take no more than half an hour.

Meanwhile, Sliwinski lingered at La Cisampo. When it was time for the program, he suggested that they should all listen to the BBC. De Prévaux certainly didn't expect his message to be broadcast that same evening, so when he suddenly heard: *"Un message important. . . . J'embrasse ma Lotka chérie. . . . Je répète: J'embrasse ma Lotka chérie,"* he was most impressed by F2's efficiency and rapidity. Extremely moved, with tears in his eyes, the French naval captain stood to attention in front of the reserve lieutenant in the Polish Army.

Neither de Prévaux nor Sliwinski had any doubt that the message did indeed come from the French Free Forces and that de Gaulle was aware that the former commander of the *Duguay-Trouin* had rallied to his cause. A year later, however, there began to be some doubt about whether F2 was in fact affiliated to the Gaullist movement. When the three main Resistance movements merged into what became known as the MUR (United Resistance Movements), F2 remained on its own, and the information it gathered continued to reach the British intelligence service and not the BCRA (the Free French Intelligence Service). In Sliwinski's view, F2's formal attachment to BCRA was not indispensable, seeing that his chiefs had once again assured him that the work done by his network would be considered as services in the Resistance. As for Havard, he felt perfectly at home in F2 and strongly disapproved of the methods of BCRA.

But de Prévaux demanded precise guarantees. In March 1943, during the reorganization of the network following the Wehrmacht's occupation of the southern zone, he announced in a telegram (March 6, 1943) that his cooperation with F2 would be only provisional until he received the assurance that he was registered as being in the permanent service of General de Gaulle. Such insistence alerted the Polish intelligence services, who were eager to secure de Prévaux's permanent cooperation. They asked their British colleagues to do what they could to get de Gaulle's consent. But the British response, which was passed on to de Prévaux, threw a monkey wrench in the works: they wanted to make him a member of General Giraud's staff.

The British, in fact, saw General Giraud, who had been installed in Algiers by the Americans in December 1942, as a more docile colleague and a more malleable representative of France in its struggle against the occupier than the intransigent General de Gaulle. The Second Polish Bureau, too, enjoyed excellent relations with the services that depended on Giraud, and were only too thankful when Giraud came to the fore. Thus the Poles and the British were in complete agreement that de Gaulle should be bypassed.

Or rather, that they should go on doing so. For the Giraud business lifted a corner of the veil concealing the subterfuge of which both de Prévaux and Sliwinski were the victims. They believed in good faith that the telegrams they radioed to the second Polish Bureau in London reached the Free French, whereas in reality they never got any further than the British intelligence service. They were not the only ones the famous MI6 had duped. Rygor Slowikowski, for example, who had created the bases of the Tudor network at Saint-Jean-de-Luz in 1940, and who went on to found his own network in Algiers, later discovered that he was in fact working for the British intelligence service. . . . In their pragmatic way, the British made use of whatever (good) agents they could find, even if they were working for others and even if they had to corrupt them. And they had the financial means to do so. Moreover, they had "normal" relations with General Sikorski and the legal Polish government-in-exile in London, but turbulent relations with de Gaulle. "The Polish government, which was already operating an important network of agents, with efficient radio links, had agreed to pass on any information it might receive to the Special Intelligence Services (SIS). . . . In January 1941 the Polish Second Bureau became the only link that could pass on this material and receive British requests for information." Finally, and above all, the British were anxious to remain as preeminent in the gathering and utilization of intelligence as they were in the conduct of the war. In short, they were not sorry to be able to keep to themselves all the extremely valuable information sent by F2. Added to these political considerations was the traditional rivalry between secret services, and also the fact that the Polish intelligence services had been operating long before the French had set up BCRA. Everything conspired to keep de Gaulle ignorant of the work of F2.

If we consider the resistants' motivations and the results they achieved, this was not too serious. After all, the first thing F2's agents wanted was to fight the Germans, never mind who with. Most of them were in any case not troubled by the idea of having to choose between de Gaulle and Giraud. And surely the most important thing was that the information they provided should help the Allies, and therefore help them to victory against the invader? On these two counts, they were not deceived.

But de Prévaux had indeed been duped, and more than once: messages had been transmitted by the BBC as if they had been sent by the Free French. Not only the first one that had been decisive in making him commit himself—*"J'embrasse ma Lotka chérie"*—but others that were supposed to confirm de Gaulle's agreement.

When it was suggested that he rally to Giraud, Jacques had very firmly replied that he fully appreciated the offer, and would be delighted to accept it as soon as the warring movements had come to an understanding. If they didn't, and in the meantime, he categorically insisted that his service should be counted as being for de Gaulle. (Telegram no. 53 from Lubicz,

April 8, 1943.) Nothing could have been clearer. To give him satisfaction, the British afterwards had a new message broadcast on the BBC French service: "France knows that you are working for her, and thanks you." How could he doubt that it emanated from the Free French? It seemed obvious to every listener that the BBC's "French program," preceded by contributions from de Gaulle or his spokesman Maurice Schumann, issued from the Free French—although this was not the case.

Yet de Prévaux was still not reassured. Sliwinski, who had been arrested in December 1942 but had escaped in September 1943, was to go to England. Jacques asked him to go and see Admiral Thierry d'Argenlieu, now commander in chief of the Free French Naval Forces, and also his friend Pierre Viénot, who, having joined de Gaulle after he had escaped, had just been appointed by the CFLN (French Committee for National Liberation) as their London ambassador. De Prévaux also entrusted him with a letter to Viénot. Dated November 1, 1943, he first of all wrote of his pride in working within the Resistance: "The choice I had to make at the beginning of this year was very difficult. Either I had to stay here in the same business which was starting to prosper again, or come and join you. But I can't regret it because my conscience is clear: I have a feeling of duty done and work achieved."

At the end of 1942, de Prévaux had indeed once again been tempted by the idea of joining the FNFL (Free French Naval Forces). That was where he belonged: before anything else he was a staff officer, and anyway, it was in order to join de Gaulle in London that he had got in touch with F2 a year before. And now, in the autumn of 1942, the General Staff was undergoing a complete reorganization and being fleshed out. There were posts to be filled, and not just any posts. After the sensational resignation of Vice Admiral Muselier in March, following a clash with de Gaulle, the post of Commander of the FNFL had been given to Philippe Auboyneau. Without wishing to cast doubt on Auboyneau's abilities, de Prévaux had observed that he himself had more seniority—Auboyneau was ten years his junior—and that consequently the post was his by right.

Moreover, the BCRA wanted to employ him, or at least to test his capacities. Colonel Pierre Fourcaud, one of the chief secret agents of the Free French, a professional, had noticed that he had joined the Resistance and appreciated what he knew of Jacques' work in F2. He had spoken to London of de Prévaux. His case had been considered at the highest level, since he had been the subject of a discussion between Admiral Auboyneau and Colonel Billotte, who was the chief of de Gaulle's personal staff and in charge of their relations with the BCRA. They had finally decided to work with him occasionally. De Prévaux would first be "used on the spot after a short stay here," "here" meaning London. Contact with him was to be made by d'Astier de la Vigerie, one of the founders of the Libération movement and its then head, who as it happened was due to go to France in November. Vox was to come to England by submarine, together with the ambassador René Massigli, the future commissioner for foreign affairs. But the submarine operation was postponed, and the series of arrests which, in December, was to decapitate F2, made Jacques change his mind and agree to stay in France, where he was more useful.

A difficult choice, as he explained to Viénot, to whom he admitted his concern about the General Staff of the Free French Naval Forces. "Yet I am sometimes overcome with nostalgia for my former métier, and I would like all those with you who are still active in it at least to be sure . . . that my absence is not really an absence." He tells himself he is certain that Viénot has been mentioning his name and reminding people "for the present and for the future" of the existence of the captain who made the right choice, indeed, yet is so far away from his general staff that he can't be sure of having received express orders. He asks Viénot to speak to Argenlieu about him: "I would like to know that I haven't been forgotten."

Unfortunately, Sliwinski didn't get to England until June or July of the following year, 1944. He introduced himself to his superiors in the Polish Second Bureau, and naïvely informed them of his mission to Viénot and Thierry d'Argenlieu.

Their reaction came as a great shock to him: they strictly forbade him to have any contact whatsoever with the representatives of the Free French. This order can no doubt be explained by the habitual reflex of intelligence services, to erect barriers between each unit and prevent horizontal contacts. They must also have feared the sudden disclosure of their stratagem: how would an excellent agent like Sliwinski react if these eminent associates of de Gaulle were to tell him that the Free French had never heard of de Prévaux's services in the Resistance? So Sliwinski found himself being forbidden by Lieutenant Colonel Langelfeld to deliver the messages de Prévaux had entrusted to him.

How little did he know this man, a total rebel to all authority, if he thought he was going to comply. Sliwinski disobeyed the order, thereby incurring the penalties for indiscipline, and set about meeting the men the letters were addressed to. But he was out of luck. Pierre Viénot died of a heart attack before he managed to see him, and Thierry d'Argenlieu was away. Finally Sliwinski wrote to him, and sent a note to Lieutenant Commander Schilling, the head of security of the French fleet in Great Britain. And that was when he discovered what was going on.

Although Schilling knew de Prévaux, he didn't know that he was working for the Resistance. And when Sliwinski tried to get his agents' services authorized so that they could benefit from promotion and pensions on the same terms as the members of the Free French fighting units, he was told that the services rendered by F2 were "not automatically" recognized by the French authorities as services to Free France. It wasn't until September 30, 1944 that an agreement signed in Paris by Colonel Manuel, number two in the BCRA, and Colonel Lesniak, head of Polish intelligence, granted the French agents in F2 terms similar to those of the agents in the BCRA.

It is true that at the Liberation de Prévaux's work was recognized by the Gaullist government, since he was awarded the Croix de la Libération and promoted to Commander in the Legion of Honor. But his name is still barely known, and does not adorn any ship in the French fleet.

There are several reasons for this. In the first place, it has to be recognized that the French Navy was long reluctant to say anything good about the work of the resistants. And then, de Prévaux had fought his battles in the shadows, far away from military headquarters and from his comrades serving in the Free French Naval Forces, and they knew nothing of his exploits. The men who were later to become the political leaders of the Fourth Republic had been companions of de Gaulle in London, and de Prévaux did not belong to their milieu. When he and his wife were gone, there was nobody to keep their memory alive, since their family preferred "to forget the tragedy." As a result of this silence, Jacques and Lotka were gradually expunged from history.

17

A SIMPLE INFORMER

May 1942, at the de Prévaux's house, La Cisampo. It was a beautiful evening. From their terrace they could see the lights of Pramousquier below and, in the distance, the sea. The Pascalis had come for a drink and been invited to stay on for dinner. Lotka had managed to track down a few bottles of wine, and Jacques, who had been in Nice "on business," had brought back enough food to make a meal worthy of the name. This was a godsend, because provisions were hard to come by in the Var. Finding meat or fresh produce was a real headache. There was always the well-known Polish woman in Toulon, but all she had left was sardines and tomato purée. As for the mysterious sailor who specialized in oil and pasta, after lengthy bargaining he would only come up with ridiculously small quantities, such as one pound of coffee and one bar of chocolate—to be shared with the Pascalis. Things were so bad that Lotka had to appeal to her parents to send her butter and cakes from Paris.

The larder was often empty. Worse still, the de Prévaux had serious financial problems—although that was nothing new. Admittedly an officer suspended from the active list still had his pay, but it was without the allowances, in particular the one that made it possible to offset the expenses of having to pay rent for two homes: his permanent residence and his accommodation in the place where he was posted. Moreover, Blandine had just managed to get her alimony taken at the source from this reduced pay. There wasn't a great deal left. Unpaid bills accumulated and were followed in due course by final demands.

De Prévaux then decided to go into business. He had been offered the position of president of a company yet to be founded, and he could already see himself thriving, and lavishing on Lotka the dresses and jewels her beauty deserved. The idea came from a man called Roger Samuel, a chemical engineer from Nice, who manufactured substitute household cleaning materials such as shoe polish, scouring powder, furniture polish. In that period of shortages and rationing it looked as if there would be a huge market for them. Substitutes of all sorts, ersatz sugar, oils containing no fat, or almost none, had already become familiar staples. Jacques immersed himself in manuals of commercial law, drafted the statutes of a limited company called *Société de produits alimentaires et ménagers de remplacement,* SPAM for short, and filed an application for a license at the prefecture. At the beginning of the month he had rented offices on the rue Pasteur in Cannes. But the company didn't get started until the following year. The license was at first refused on the grounds that the application was too vague, giving no details of chemical components or manufacturing procedures. A more technical dossier was required.

But on that May evening life was good. Sitting in a deckchair, Jacques was vividly describing the events of his trip. He had at last finished with the tortures of the dentist and had a brand-new set of dentures that made him look younger. Lotka had taken a canvas folding chair out to a corner of the terrace, where she could see Jacques, and was looking at him as she softly played the accordion. A typical picture of a group of friends quietly gossiping as they drank their apéritifs in the garden.

And the conversation was indeed only about banal subjects, for a couple of notorious collaborators lived in the adjoining villa. The de Prévaux had very few trusted friends in the neighborhood, apart from Colonel Pierre Fourcaud, one of the chief secret agents of the Free French, a professional but something of an adventurer. He had been sent by the BCRA in August 1941 to sound out Admiral de Laborde, the commander in chief of the Toulon seagoing forces, on what his attitude would be in the event of a German attack on the French fleet, and—a more delicate question—whether he might eventually join the Free French Naval Forces. Fourcaud and Jacques had discussed what to do to get in touch with the admiral. They had noticed that every evening he changed into civilian clothes, got into a civilian dinghy and crossed the harbor to go home to his house in Tamaris. "I followed him," Fourcaud recalled, "I looked through the window of his villa and rang his doorbell. What a dressing-down I got! De Prévaux doubled up with laughter when I told him. He didn't think I'd have the cheek to confront Laborde." Fourcaud had indeed boldly introduced himself under his real name, revealing his rank and his job with de Gaulle, and point-blank announced the reason for his unorthodox approach. Admiral de Laborde not only threw him out but also informed Darlan of the presence of the BCRA's emissary.

Fourcaud still had a vivid recollection of the couple who had been his neighbors for a few months. "De Prévaux was a very well-known and very well-liked naval captain. He was certainly on his way to becoming an admiral. But the men in London had ganged up, they had made themselves a new naval ministry on the banks of the Thames. And they ought to have given de Prévaux a rank that corresponded with his reputation. Because in Toulon, he was irreplaceable. . . . She—she was bewitching. They made a magnificent couple." For Jacques and Lotka, Fourcaud represented a breath of fresh London air; they asked him to describe life in Gaullist circles. But their contacts had to remain discreet. Fourcaud was under surveillance by two police inspectors who had moved in with the baker in Cavalaire, about ten

kilometers from Pramousquier. They never spotted the de Prévaux.

Dr. Raymond Leibovici was another frequent visitor to La
Cisampo. This militant communist had been sent by Franc
Tireurs et Partisans in Saint-Tropez. With Villon, Kriegel-Valri-
mont, Rol-Tanguy and others, he was a member of the Committee for Action against Deportation (CAD), and his unit
later became part of the maquis in the Brigade des Maures. A
mutual friend put him in touch with Jacques, who described his
time in Alexandria and "how he had ditched Admiral Godfroy
in order to go back to France and serve." Leibovici and de Prévaux agreed to exchange any interesting information they obtained. "I remember him as an admirable man," Leibovici later
said, "and her as a tall, likeable bicycle-courier whose courage
I admired."

The other friend of the couple was more conspicuous. Visits
to La Cisampo by Joseph Kessel and his girlfriend Germaine
Sablon did not go unnoticed. Alcohol flowed freely, even more
so than usual, and while Jacques and Lotka could drink to excess without ever getting drunk, Kessel tended to become up-
roarious when in his cups. There was then a considerable
racket, which disturbed the neighbors. One day when Jacques
was trying to persuade his friend to keep his voice down by
showing him the good French citizens on the watch in the next-
door garden, the writer dashed out on the terrace and, among
general hilarity, bawled out: "Vive Hitler!"

That kind of outburst would have been out of place that
evening with the Pascalis. Around the table, with the windows
carefully shut, they talked shop. Gaston Pascalis (Sag) was F2's
cryptographer; he transcribed reports and telegrams with the
aid of the grids and tables contained in a big book hidden in the
garden. When, a year later, in June 1943, little Aude de Prévaux
was christened in Opio, Pascalis stood in for her godfather: they

had chosen Sliwinski, although he had been arrested and was then in prison. As for Mathilde Pascalis, it was by pure chance that she and Lotka had met in the Midi. They had known each other in 1938 in Paris at Louis Philippe, a little beauty parlor where Lotka had worked, run by Eva Peralla, a childhood friend of Mathilde.

The two women discussed the curious fate that had led the Polish émigrée from Vionnet's glittering salons to the obscure task of clandestine courier. "I could easily have imagined becoming a cleaning woman one day, but certainly not a spy," Lotka once said casually, with a laugh. She knew how to speak lightly of serious matters. "But that's what you were made for," Jacques replied admiringly.

Lotka (Kalo) had just come back from a difficult mission, and her nonchalance concealed enormous relief. She had brought from Paris, crossing the demarcation line unscathed, a big suitcase full of papers for Sliwinski. In theory, thanks to the quasi-professional organization of F2, everything should have proceeded without a hitch. Its false papers were foolproof— since they joined the network, Lotka had received a splendid genuine false identity card in the name of Jacqueline Chebrou, née Pajot, living in Laval. The network of frontier guides was absolutely reliable, and in particular the vital link: the bookseller on the rue Carnot in Monceau-les-Mines, Madame Forest, whose bicycle was much used in those days.

Yet Jacques was still trembling at the risks she had run. Even dressed in a hideous raincoat and with her head covered by a shabby scarf, Lotka didn't go unnoticed. Her height and her model's walk inevitably drew attention to her. Even more dangerous was the slight, and charming, central European accent she still had, which might arouse curiosity. In short, she wasn't really secret agent material. . . . Never mind the fact that a grain of sand can always wreck a machine—arrive ten minutes late for a rendezvous and everything falls through. And while it is possible, if you are arrested, to get rid of a message, possibly a report typed on onionskin paper, how can you spirit away a suitcase full of compromising documents? Getting it through had been a remarkable achievement, and earned Lotka the Croix de la Vaillance, awarded by the Polish government in London on September 12, 1942.

Lotka's first work in the network had been as Jacques' secretary. Then she demanded more dangerous jobs, and soon became an agent entrusted with special missions, and ultimately chief courier of the F2 network. In place of the classic system of postboxes, the network preferred to use the courier, which they found safer, since their liaison agents always met their contacts in different places, as for instance the second compartment of the 10.18 railcar traveling between Toulon and Bandol. Lotka made many journeys on the Nice–Toulon–Marseille line all through 1942 — in fact, until she became pregnant. She also took the network's reports to Lyon, several hundred pages, plus maps and plans of the disposition of the enemy's troops. The orders were that the courier must await instructions, which implied staying overnight somewhere in Lyon, preferably with a concierge — the best way of being sure that she wouldn't denounce you. As for her "special missions," some really were special, like the time she accompanied Sliwinski to Paris and they pretended to be lovers in order to avoid awkward questions. Most missions were both important and dangerous: liaising with the Americans, escorting Allied soldiers . . .

You couldn't allow yourself to be frightened. But Lotka, who had been distraught when she had no letters from Jacques, was a woman who could always rise to the occasion. Unable to cope with minor irritations, in despair over some trivial domestic problem, she found she had hidden depths when the situation was serious. It was as if, all of a sudden, another Lotka had taken over from the usual Lotka, one who made instant decisions and acted with resolution and without fear. Her only comment on her latest successful exploit was: "I was a bit worried about whether I'd be able to cross the line with that great big suitcase. . . . " Pascal, who after Sliwinski's arrest replaced him at the head of F2, wrote in a memorandum recommending Lotka for the Médaille de la Résistance (which she was awarded on June 5, 1945): "In every one of her missions she showed extraordinary sangfroid, exemplary courage and remarkable tenacity."

For his part, Jacques threw all his energy and organizational skills into his work for F2. At first he was recruited as a simple informer, one of the three hundred subordinate agents whose job was to collect information on the activities of the enemy troops.

They had been carefully chosen according to extremely strict criteria: discipline, exactitude, discretion and efficiency. Each was responsible for a specific sector; one would observe the movements of soldiers on a particular route, with the number of motorized vehicles, their insignia and flags; another would note any work done on a particular fortification, or the slightest modification of a minefield, real or false. A railroad worker would copy the dockets listing the train loads. Someone else would keep an eye on supplies of fresh food, and another on the movements of men on leave.

This meticulous work ended as a mass of information piled up on the desks of the heads of each sector, one for every large town. At the beginning, F2 operated only in Toulon, Marseille, La Ciotat and Nice, but the network later expanded to cover the whole Mediterranean coast and was divided into subnetworks, subsectors and other administrative units. The heads of the sectors must not pass on to the upper levels any information that was not completely reliable or could not be immediately exploited. It was their job to check, sort, classify and summarize the material collected by their agents. This amounted to an enormous workload, which they had to complete in two days at the most, twice a month, and in secrecy. Among other things, this meant that they had to move their "exchange" every two weeks, because their premises—an office or just a room—must on no account be identified. They were crammed full of documents, maps, reports from the different agents, and everything that couldn't be destroyed. And, of course, they had to keep their archives for their next report.

Each head of sector passed on his report to the central bureau in Nice, where the network's main report was compiled. The most urgent information was sent by radio. The network's report, which roughly covered a two-week period, reached London by different routes. It was taken by frontier guides and sent via Spain and Gibraltar; simultaneously it went via Vichy, where it was handed over to the U.S. naval attaché. Later it went via Switzerland, where the intermediary was "Monseigneur," a Swiss priest who lived in Grenoble. This report was a voluminous document of several hundred pages (soon to be microphotographed with a Leica), with detailed maps and sketches, giving such specific information about the army of occupation as their battle formation and movements; their fortifications, their airfields; their antiaircraft sites; their development of new materials; the results of air raids on their positions; their naval bases, shipyards, arsenals, coastal fortifications; the movements of their merchant navy; their road and rail transport. And finally, it contained information on the production, the work force and the output of the munitions factories.

Apart from a coding office, a department for forging false papers, and its couriers, F2 had a political sector, whose job it was to make contacts with representatives of neutral countries in Vichy. The network was thus able to tell London what German diplomatic activity was going on behind the scenes in Vichy. The political sector also served as a link between F2 and other Resistance movements. In spite of security considerations, the networks were not strictly compartmentalized. They often exchanged their agents, according to the missions to be accomplished; many of those who supplied information to F2 were members of the armed action or sabotage groups. As F2 was the first network to have radio contacts with London, it continued to serve as an intermediary. The reports it transmitted always contained messages from other groups or networks, requests for parachute drops or funds, and F2 also offered them the use of their infrastructure of escape routes via Gibraltar or Switzerland.

A network composed of amateurs, F2 operated with a professionalism that many intelligence services might well envy. Gaston Havard remembered all the precautions they took in recruiting their agents and the emphasis they laid on exactitude, since their rendezvous were most often simple meetings on a given itinerary. He also remembered that they were used to searching each other: "An agent must never have anything compromising on him. . . . hence, everyone had the right and the duty to search his subordinate's pockets and wallet periodically." This routine had the added advantage that they knew exactly what an agent had on him if he was arrested, which made further arrests less likely. "When I look back at all those precautions, which some of us found excessive," Havard wrote proudly, "I can't help thinking that they are probably the main reason why we suffered no arrests in Toulon from 1940 right up to the Liberation."

After having proved himself as a simple informer for three months, and therefore having agreed to have his pockets searched, de Prévaux was officially accepted as a member of F2 in April 1942, as deputy to Sliwinski with special responsibility for the navy. He was made head of one of the two sectors in Toulon, Havard and Brun being jointly responsible for the other. He chose Lévy-Rueff (Vir) as his second in command.

But the German invasion of the free zone was soon to complicate the task of the resistants.

18
FIGHTING IN THE SHADOWS

In the autumn of 1942, the Wehrmacht was preparing to invade the southern zone. This would mean the disarmament of the armistice troops quartered south of the demarcation line, and the seizure by the Germans of the French Fleet in Toulon—Operation Lila. The Allies wanted to find out what the reaction of the French Navy would be. Would it simply surrender to the Germans and hand over its ships without firing a shot? Could it be hoped, in spite of the bitter memory of Mers el-Kébir, that some of the ships would decide to join the British fleet? How many? Which ones? Could they at least count on an order for sabotage being given, to prevent the enemy fleet seizing the hundred-odd ships based there?

In July or August 1942, F2 received a dispatch from London, asking for a report on the likely attitude of Admiral de Laborde and the commanding officers of the vessels—among them three battleships, seven cruisers and fifteen submarines. De Prévaux, who knew the navy well, and also the state of mind prevalent in military circles in Toulon, had to admit that the majority of officers were more interested in playing tennis than in carrying on the fight. In a prophetic report, he bluntly concluded that in no case would the officers of the French Navy agree to fight with the British. The best they could hope for was sabotage.

Yet it took subterfuge, or the clever exploitation of the difficulties of communication, to bring it about. How it happened is described in the *History of the Azur Network.*

> On 27 November at five in the morning, [German] armored cars arrived at the arsenal . . . Their intention was to board the ships which were all alongside. . . . The sailors refused to allow them on board. During this time the telephone was never idle; Vichy was being asked for orders. But the telephone exchange was controlled by our agents. One of them realized that Vichy was giving the order to surrender, so he cut them off. He told Vichy that the Germans had cut the line to the admiral, and he told the admiral that the line to Vichy had been cut.

The Vichy premier Pierre Laval had in fact boasted that he was negotiating, and had given the order to "avoid all incidents"—in other words, to abandon the fleet to the enemy without firing a shot—and he had added that the latest instructions canceled those given previously—that's to say the secret orders for sabotage given by Darlan on June 22, 1940. Since he didn't receive the new instructions issued by Laval, Admiral de Laborde finally carried out the June 1940 instructions, and gave the order for sabotage. Just four submarines decided to put out to sea, but one of them hit a minefield and had to return to port. The three others, the *Casabianca,* the *Glorieux* and the *Marsouin,* managed to reach North Africa. Two thirds of the fleet was sabotaged, with varying results. Some ninety ships sank and couldn't be recovered by the Germans, and only about forty were handed over with their arms and munitions intact, and sometimes as a bonus their well-filled storerooms too.

"Our crew surpassed itself during this day of sabotage," this same *History* says, explaining how the Toulon sector of F2 had distributed the work among its agents, demanding "thorough and almost immediate results." That same evening we knew exactly what damage had been done to each ship, and this was at a time when the Germans were intercepting any approach by land or sea. This initial information was later checked and turned out to be absolutely accurate. At the same time, the Resistance knew the strength of the Germans, the names of their units, where they were quartered, what weapons they had, the number of the vehicles and so on. The special report sent on the 28th (the day after the sabotage) by the six A.M. train was a model of clarity and precision.

It's easy to understand that the British were satisfied with the work of F2—they had already appreciated de Prévaux's lucid report on the state of mind of the Toulon fleet.

This was also one of the main reasons why the British Navy pressed for him to be awarded the Distinguished Service Order. It is a decoration that is rarely given to a foreigner; during the war only eight French sailors were judged worthy of it for services to the Allies. On January 30, 1943 de Prévaux was the very first to receive it, after barely nine months of work already recognized as exceptional.

It was then, at the end of 1942, that F2 ran the greatest risks. With the occupation of the southern zone—the Wehrmacht had crossed the demarcation line on November 11—the enemy was now established in Marseille, Toulon and Nice. The railway stations were under surveillance, the streets and squares were no longer safe, and agents had to double their precautions when transmitting the information it had become more perilous to gather. But while the Germans had taken over the Toulon arsenal and the naval aviation bases, it was the Italian army that occupied the region, a relatively painless occupation. However, the end of the fiction of the "free zone" reinforced both patriotic feelings and the repression of the Resistance.

London had warned F2 of the imminence of the occupation and advised it to evacuate its principal agents. Almost every one of them refused categorically. It was out of the question to abandon the fight. But it was not only a matter of courage; the network had to go on operating, and it was feared that the German and Italian counterespionage services might be able to destroy it. That was when its leaders took a series of decisions aimed at making the network even more clandestine. Agents who had been identified and threatened were sent away at once; the Poles, in particular, had to leave the zone. The archives were reduced to the bare minimum, the more exposed sectors were dissolved, and the rest had to prepare themselves to work autonomously. F2's command post had to withdraw to the Grenoble-Chambéry region; a rendezvous of the chief leaders was planned for January 6 in Grenoble.

In spite of these security measures, the Germans, who had been tipped off by informers recruited among "good French citizens" and by a handful of moles infiltrated into the network, succeeded in arresting a few agents. Most of them narrowly escaped the traps set for them and managed to let their contacts know when a rendezvous had to be canceled or when their mailbox had been discovered, and were able to destroy or move compromising papers. None of the agents arrested ever revealed anything whatsoever, some at the cost of their lives—for example, George Makowski (Gin), de Prévaux's right-hand man in Nice. In July 1943, warned by Vox that he had been spotted, Gin still insisted on going home in order to destroy everything that could compromise the network. "While he was burning the last of his papers the Gestapo, accompanied by the carabinieri, broke down the door. He had always said he was afraid he might talk under torture, and just as the carabinieri were about to grab him he jumped out of the window—he was on the sixth floor. . . ." Auguste-Henry Brun, the trade unionist, Havard's unwavering associate, was also caught. In Nîmes he fell into a trap set for the Freemasons, who were to have given him some information. He was tortured and deported.

The Germans soon caught up with F2's withdrawal strategy. A few days before the network "moved house" to Grenoble, the

German counterespionage services managed to get their hands on its leader. On the day after Christmas, the Abwehr, alerted by a double agent, organized a roundup in Nice jointly with the Italian secret services. Some thirty people were arrested, Sliwinski among them. At first he gave the carabinieri the slip, but after a brief gun battle in the streets of Nice he was recaptured and imprisoned.

The network was left well and truly leaderless. But it wasn't wiped out. The agents were tortured but gave no names away, and the rest of the organization remained intact, complete with its informers, its equipment, its fifteen transmitting stations and its codes. Even Sliwinski was replaced without difficulty. Vincent Rozwadowski (Pascal), whom Sliwinski had chosen to succeed him in the new clandestine setup, simply took over a few weeks earlier than planned. It was at this point that de Prévaux made the crucial decision to stay in France. He had devoted himself to his mission as intelligence agent within F2 as conscientiously as he undertook every job he did, but it was still his intention to go to London and again take his place on the staff, naturally with the Free French Naval Forces. His career pointed him toward de Gaulle. At the beginning of 1943 the FNFL still contained very few flag officers, and the naval General Staff needed to be reinforced. The command of the naval war was a highly interesting job, which de Prévaux considered himself capable of doing. Not to mention that now he was fifty-five it was probably his last chance to rise in rank. . . . But the wave of arrests that had just hit F2 threatened the very existence of the network; they had to find more leaders to reconstruct the organization and continue their work. Jacques might long to join the FNFL, but he knew in his heart that he was more useful in Toulon than in London. If he left now, he would be running away from the battle and abandoning his endangered companions—in short, deserting. The values he had inherited from his Catholic education (duty) and from his military training (honor) required him to carry on the fight in France. He made the decision without hesitation, but with death in his heart: it meant giving up the navy and his profession, living with the permanent risk of being denounced and arrested, and dragging Lotka with him. She was finally expecting a baby. They were both overjoyed, but neither dreamed for an instant of abandoning the struggle.

F2 was immediately put on hold—out of prudence, certainly, but also because they had to renew their contacts with London and convince the Polish General Staff that the security conditions could once again be guaranteed. This was done by February, and work was then resumed, with a new organization and, above all, with stricter security rules. For at the beginning of 1943 the struggle within France had intensified. When the Nazis started to send French workers to forced labor in Germany, the Maquis was beginning to get organized, armed networks multiplied and their activity was stepped up. The Germans, who were suffering their first military defeat on the Soviet front, fell back to their "Fortress Europe," and redoubled their efforts to obtain total freedom of action on French territory. Their counterespionage forces became more powerful, and with the efficient aid of the militia checks, searches, roundups and arrests became mFore frequent. F2 had to adapt to more difficult working conditions and at the same time provide fuller information more rapidly. For instance, they had to let the Allies know very quickly how efficient their air raids had been so that they could make their aim more accurate, not only to make them more effective but also to spare civilian victims. They had to tell them—preferably before they had been completed—the whereabouts of German fortifications along the Atlantic and Mediterranean coasts, indicate all the movements of enemy units in the fighting ports, the ships in dry dock, and the dates when those that had been repaired would leave the shipyards. The aim of all this was clear: they had to provide London with everything that could be known about the enemy that could facilitate the Allied landing. Therefore, the network must be kept operating at full strength until D day.

This aim was fully achieved. On August 16, 1946, General de Lattre de Tassigny declared at Draguignan: "I want to stress here that the accuracy, importance and intelligence of the information provided to Allied Command by the Resistance of this region was one of the determining factors of the success of our landing. The battle order and movements of the enemy, the emplacement of their units, defense organizations and batteries, were all shown in detail. There was not a single concrete road block, not a machine-gun support, not a minefield whose location and even size had not been specified by the Resistance. . . . "

Havard remembered what he had been told by an Allied soldier from the armored division who had been wounded at the battle of Toulon: "He told me how surprised he and his comrades were when, a few hours before they landed on the beach at Saint-Raphaël, each tank was given a copy of the ordnance survey map of the region on which all the minefields—real or false—were marked. He assured me that no tank had been blown up by a mine between Saint-Raphaël and Toulon." And de Lattre concluded: "Who will ever be able to do justice to the sterling qualities of these men who, with calm, smiling heroism and at the risk of their lives, moved about among the enemy installations and transmitted their information, either by the clandestine radios the Gestapo were so assiduously tracking down, or, eluding the vigilance of the German launches, by taking it out to sea, to a submarine from Africa?"

19

THE ARREST OF THE LEITNERS

Lotka had been worried about her parents for a long time, and also about her sister Mania and her brother-in-law. Mania, seven years younger than Lotka, was the only child who had stayed quietly at home. She had delighted her parents by agreeing to a real Jewish marriage, arranged by a matchmaker. Her betrothed, Kouba Distenfeld, was a rich furrier, twenty years her senior, and a talented violinist. When the Distenfelds unobtrusively crossed the demarcation line in August 1942, Lotka, who loved them, begged Jacques to find them a safe haven in the Midi. They settled in Nice, and the two couples met, wrote to each other, encouraged each other to put up with the difficulty of the times, and shared the few provisions they managed to get hold of.

Their parents were then alone in Paris. Their little haberdashery, at 78 rue Legendre in the 17th arrondissement, had been closed down because they were Jews, and their savings and what their children could spare them were their only means of support. Their son Jacques sent money orders; their son Willy, who was an insurance agent and hypnotist in Châtellerault, regularly brought them a suitcase full of eggs, butter and vegetables. Their oldest son, Milan, who had been a prisoner of war, was now back in Paris, but he and his wife, Jeanne, didn't go to see them as often as they would have liked.

Bit by bit, the net of anti-Semitic persecution closed in on them. They should have left Paris, but where could they go? At their age—sixty-eight and seventy-three—they found any sort of move arduous, especially at a time when public transportation was so chaotic. In the countryside, they would too easily be identified as Jews to remain hidden for long. Besides, their identity cards were rubber-stamped JEW in capital letters.

Lotka was extremely worried about them. The pathetic letters she received from time to time, sometimes in French and sometimes in Yiddish, referred to the dangers threatening them since they had been forced to wear the yellow star, but said they were getting resigned to them. "We've been through some difficult times," Bertha wrote, "but things are getting a little better. There are some new roundups of foreigners under 65. Fortunately I'm 68. But who knows? Perhaps it'll happen to me some day." Even in their distress, they still found the strength to worry about Lotka's health—knowing she was pregnant—and to send her parcels of cakes and butter, which were unobtainable in the Midi, asking her to return the packaging. Lotka wanted to go to Paris to see them but they wouldn't let her. In her condition, such a journey was unthinkable. They were only too happy to know that their two daughters were safe in the Midi, and were profoundly grateful to Jacques for looking after Mania and Kouba.

On February 11, 1943, the police descended on rue Legendre. They had to knock hard to wake the concierge—it was two in the morning. Madame Lelong kept her head and tried her best to persuade the inspector that he had drawn a blank. "The Leitners? My goodness, I haven't seen them for quite a few days. They must have gone. If they hadn't, I'd have seen them, believe me. They must have gone, actually they were talking about it...." The courageous woman was so categorical that the police were convinced. Even so, they went up and rang the Leitner's doorbell, as a matter of form.

Their eyes wide open in the dark, huddled up in their bed, Bertha and Isidore listened, shivering, to the approaching footsteps and the more and more violent blows on the door. Isidore whispered: "I've locked it, all we have to do is not answer and they'll think there's no one here." But in turning the key with his trembling hand he had broken it in the lock, thus revealing to the police that there was indeed someone inside the flat. It only remained for them to break the door down.

"Your mother," Madame Lelong wrote to Lotka, "was very brave, not a tear on her face. And your father, who lost heart for a moment when the inspector and the policeman first arrived, very soon got a grip on himself. You see what great strength elderly people can have." Jeanne was tormented with remorse: only a day or two earlier she had begged her parents-in-law not to go on sleeping in their flat, but they had said: "We'll wait until they come once, and then we'll go." She ought to have insisted.

Isidore and Bertha were first interned in the Drancy transit camp. Their children rallied around them. They were each allowed one three-kilogram parcel per week; Willy sent the ingredients for Jeanne to make into restorative cakes and jam. At first there was still a very slim hope that they might remain at Drancy in the hospital, but, as Jeanne wrote to Lotka; "up to the age of 75, and sometimes even older, you're sent further away." To Auschwitz.

The Leitners left on March 2, 1943, in convoy number 49. Their last message was a postcard written to the concierge, posted from the Drancy camp, with these few lines in pencil: "Chère Madame, my husband and I are leaving tomorrow morning for an unknown destination. We are keeping up our courage. Will you be kind enough to tell my friend in rue Saint-Placide [Jeanne]. I won't write to my children, and I shall be grateful if you won't write to them either. Thank you for everything you have done for me. With my best wishes, Bertha Leitner."

No one knows whether they reached Auschwitz. Many of the deportees died in the special trains, and on arrival the weakest and oldest were immediately eliminated.

Mania and Kouba Distenfeld were arrested a year later. They left on April 13, 1944, in convoy number 71, one of the last to deliver Jews to Auschwitz. Neither they nor their parents came back.

As for Lotka, her Jewish origin never got her into trouble. In October 1941 there had been an anxious moment, though; the police were making enquiries about the Jews living in Rayol, the nearest town to Pramousquier. And the law of May 19, 1941, allowed the high commissioner for Jewish questions, Xavier Vallat, to order "the police to take every measure that is in the public interest," making no distinction between the French and foreigners. This could have meant internment. But no action followed the inquiry.

Yet the authorities knew perfectly well that Lotka was Jewish, both because she had been to Rayol to register herself as such and because of a declaration made by Jacques. A decree of June 2, 1941, had set up a census of all the Jews living in the unoccupied zone. They had to file a declaration that they were Jewish; a husband had to do this for his wife. When, in August, Jacques had received through official channels the form that all officers and civil servants had to fill in, he had purposely omitted to mention Lotka's Jewish ancestry. But a few weeks later, on October 28, he bent over backwards to ensure that a correction reached Vichy in time, a correction stating that his wife was indeed Jewish. . . . This disconcerting declaration can be explained in several different ways. By naïveté, perhaps: very many Jews had fallen into the trap of legality, of the illusion that if their papers were legally in order, however infamous the law, they would be protected against any arbitrary decision. It was probably also meant to be a clever move: de Prévaux was already in contact with Azur-F2's agents and preparing—at least, so he believed—to leave secretly for London. He may have thought it shrewd to allay possible suspicions by making a display of his bona fide honesty.

Jacques himself explained his attitude differently. Of the first declaration stating that Lotka was an Aryan, he said: "I made that mistake in the heat of the moment, in a fit of indignation and very understandable rebellion against that inquisition of the person whom I hold most dear in all the world." Of the correction, proclaiming that Lotka was indeed Jewish: "I was tortured by the lie, although I only told it as a reaction to the outrage to your dignity. . . . It had often made me feel a kind of remorse and apprehension. . . . Now I feel relief: the truth is as beautiful and gentle as you are." Moral rectitude and candor, whatever the consequences—and he must have been ware of the dangers of the clandestine fight he was engaging in—were, for de Prévaux, absolute values.

20

VOX IN DANGER

On May 15, 1943, de Prévaux took command of the subnetwork called Anne, which brought together the Toulon, Marseille and Nice sectors. Since F2 had resumed its activities after the arrest of its leader, Sliwinski, his successor, Rozwadowski (Pascal), had reorganized its structure. The Mediterranean sector, the most important, had been built into the Anne "sub-network," within which different geographical sectors were to operate. Gilbert Foury (Edwin) was the first head of Anne, but in the spring he was sent to the north of France to take over the Paris and Normandy sectors, which had been vegetating after the arrest of their principal agents. Jacques was then chosen to be the head of Anne, while his deputy, Lévy-Rueff, took on the responsibility for Toulon II.

This "promotion" meant more intensive work for de Prévaux, and above all more traveling. From his center of activities he had to go to Toulon and the Alpes-Maritimes, to Cannes and Nice. F2's command post had been established in Nice, with the radio cell, the two transmitting stations, the coding department and the secretariat, while Anne's planning department had moved to Cannes. Up till then, Jacques had had only some fifty kilometers to travel between Pramousquier and Toulon: now he had an eighty-kilometer journey to get to Nice.

It was an exhausting life. He was torn between managing

SPAM, the substitute food and household products business he had founded, running the network, and the extra care needed by Lotka, pregnant and devastated by her parents' deportation. SPAM alone would have been enough to keep him occupied; the returns from this business justified the time and energy he spent on it. De Prévaux had been on the retired list since April, and his pension was not enough for three people to live on, particularly as Blandine was still demanding her alimony and at the slightest delay threatened to take him to court for desertion of his family (his older daughter was then twenty-two). But SPAM had also turned out to be a fortuitous cover for his frequent visits to Anne's various sectors and his contacts within the network. He never traveled without a voluminous briefcase overflowing with samples of wax polish or face cream, under which his compromising documents were hidden.

Transportation was especially wearing. It wasn't unusual for him to have to spend every night in a different town, at a hotel or at one of their rented flats in Nice, Cannes or Saint-Raphaël. Since he went home to Lotka as often as he possibly could, he had to waste an unreasonable amount of time standing on a packed platform, waiting for trains running an hour late. Part of his journey consisted of a ten-kilometer bicycle ride from one station to another. Naturally, when he got to his destination he couldn't just collapse into a director's chair. As had been the case in Toulon in Havard's time, his meetings with agents and couriers took place in the street along an agreed itinerary. When Lotka read a letter from Jacques telling her: "Today I again spent most of my time walking," she knew that Vox had been working for F2.

This was more than enough to exhaust a fifty-five-year-old. Jacques, who only two years before had been hospitalized for anemia, was losing his strength—he had edema in his legs and back and was always putting off the necessary operation (he hadn't time for it). Gritting his teeth, he carried on with his travels and spent his nights organizing the network, reading his agents' reports and doing SPAM's accounts. He was happy to be once again in the state of exaltation that had been so familiar during his seagoing commands—that strange phenomenon in which, while his body felt more dead than alive, his spirit seemed to have grown wings.

But he was worried about Lotka. He more or less forced her to move house: it was absurd to go on living in the Var. He had found a villa in Opio, a few kilometers from Grasse. He would be able to return there more frequently, and not be so tired. But Lotka missed Pramousquier. She was demoralized and, with her advancing pregnancy, no longer had the distraction of difficult missions. She was feverishly preparing the baby's layette and got into a panic over trifles—problems with diapers and not enough clothes coupons. She hated being uprooted just a few weeks before the baby was due, detested "this horrible house," and couldn't stand the presence of a fellow tenant. She would never get used to Castello San Peyre.

Three months after Aude's birth, the family moved to Nice.

In the meantime, the sub-network Anne was developing rapidly under de Prévaux's energetic direction. After two months it already covered the whole Mediterranean coast between Ventimiglia and Perpignan. It had become a model network, a factory working all out to produce information. The reports he sent to London every two weeks contained up to two-hundred pages and included all the German and Italian battle formations, their coastal fortifications, the movements of their naval units, the dockyard activities and the traffic on all the airfields and railways.

F2 itself had been extended and ramified: at that time—mid-July 1943—it covered practically the whole of France, with four sub-networks which had been given charming female names: Anne, Cécile, Madeleine and Félicie. It had its parachute cells, and it had decentralized laboratories making false papers, capable of producing overnight a whole set of top-quality identity cards, ration cards, operational orders and German permits to enter military premises. Transport to England was perfectly organized. Every month at the new moon a little boat commanded by a Polish naval officer moored somewhere between Saint-Raphaël and Cannes. It came from Gibraltar to deliver equipment, pick up reports and evacuate compromised agents. The system of radio contacts, already excellent, had in the meantime been perfected: each sub-network had its own radio contact with London and a complex safety mechanism that enabled their transmitters, practically mass-produced by a "pianist" of genius, Jérôme Stroweis (Carbo), to operate to the maximum in spite of the German direction finders. The exchange even kept a radio and an operator "pianist" in reserve in case of a sudden emergency in one of the sectors.

All this was thanks to the courage of the agents who, when arrested and tortured by the Gestapo, managed not to talk, or at least to hold out for forty-eight hours. ("We considered an agent to be a hero if he held out for forty-eight hours," Havard wrote.) This was time enough for their contacts, couriers and mail drops, alerted by their nonappearance at a rendezvous, to clean out their premises and vanish into thin air. Moreover, this short time was long enough for the reserve team to take over the sector and continue the work in progress as if nothing had happened—for instance, to complete a report that had to be sent that evening. It was also thanks to luck, and to the skill of the agents who had been arrested yet still found a way to warn the others.

In June 1943, for instance, Anne and the whole of the F2 network narrowly escaped a trap set by the Gestapo. In Toulouse the sub-network Félicie had just fallen into the hands of the Germans; its agents were arrested, the enemy had got hold of its codes and reports and therefore discovered the name and address of the network's mail drop in Nice. The fate of the network hung by a thread. The Gestapo forced the head of Félicie to write a provocative letter to mislead his contacts in Nice, but he managed to insert enough clues to warn them of the danger. Headquarters were immediately alerted. De Prévaux set the security arrangements in motion: all the known Toulouse agents were sent away from Nice, and all the premises whose addresses they might know were vacated. So everything was all right? Not quite. Havard, who came from Nice every month for an exchange of views with de Prévaux, had arranged a meeting for the next day and, as it happened, at one of the houses that had been spotted. It was too late to let him know before he left Toulon, and no one knew the arrival time of his train. . . . Later Havard described how he had escaped the ambush thanks to Jacques' courage. Jacques had had no hesitation in running an enormous risk: "Counting on my well-known obsession about punctuality, Vox found a way to pass me in the street just as I got to the building (the one that had been spotted by the Gestapo) and walked straight on without stopping. So I followed him at a distance until he came to a park, where he sat down on a remote bench from which he had an unrestricted view. I checked that there really was no one else in sight, and then sat down beside him. He brought me up to date with what had happened and arranged to meet me in a safe place. And there we had our work session."

A series of well-targeted arrests, though, had confirmed the suspicion that the German intelligence services knew of the existence of F2 and were actively searching for it. Agents who had been arrested had seen pinned up on the walls of the Gestapo offices diagrams representing what the Germans imagined to be F2's organization, which they were trying unsuccessfully to demolish. The *département* of Alpes-Maritimes in particular, which included Nice, was becoming a highly dangerous zone. The network's headquarters had by then moved—and not for the last time—and been transferred from Nice into the Rhône-Alpes region, setting up its different services in Lyon, Grenoble and Chambéry.

Only the sub-network Anne stayed where it was. Leaving Nice was out of the question. The intelligence provided by Vox's sub-network was too valuable, especially at that time, the end of 1943. The war at last seemed to have taken a decisive turn in favor of the Allies, and the planned landings in Normandy and on the coast of Provence were taking shape. F2's objective was to continue to provide the information that would enable the operations to be carried out in the most favorable conditions, and to remain operational until the day of the landing. This meant that Anne must be kept in Nice until the last moment.

Yet de Prévaux was in danger. His colleagues were more and more afraid that he would be discovered. His determination to obtain as much information as possible, and to galvanize his men, drove him into setting an example by taking risks. He trusted in fate and hardly took the trouble to disguise himself. In March 1944, Rozwadowski (Pascal), the F2 leader, considered that the time had come to move him on. Everyone in the network called him Commander, and he risked being identified. Pascal was thinking of moving Vox to Lyon, to take the place of Lévy-Rueff, who had been moved from the Toulon sector when his Jewish origin put him in danger.

But it was already too late. On March 29, Vox was arrested.

The trap closed on de Prévaux on March 29, 1944. It was an ordinary working Wednesday; he had a rendezvous in Marseille with the head of the sector, Jean Bringué (Kot). He had gone there with his closest colleagues, Armand Fradin (Good) and Thérèse Bailet (Théo), and his cipher officer, Gaston Pascalis (Sag). The meeting must have been important, since all of Anne's principal agents were taking part. The question of transferring the headquarters was probably on the agenda. In arresting Vox and the other leaders of Anne in Marseille that day, the Gestapo made a great catch.

After two years' experience in a secret organization, it is inconceivable that de Prévaux had not taken all necessary precautions against the meeting being detected. The participants would all have come by different trains and routes, having made sure they were not followed, and arrived not simultaneously but one after the other, at a safe location provided with several exits. So there can be only two possible explanations of the well-informed Gestapo bursting in. Either someone had talked under torture or there was a traitor in the network. The first hypothesis was put forward by Lubicz, the head of F2, in the telegram he sent on April 14 informing London of de Prévaux's arrest: "Its cause was probably the interception of the mail sent to Vox by the Marseille sector." This was also what

Henri Stroweis (Balzac), an important agent in Lyon, said he
had been told at Montluc. One of Kot's agents had been arrested and talked, and Kot had not been warned in time. The
second hypothesis was more generally accepted by the members of the network; they thought it strange that only Mug had
escaped the raid. Shortly afterwards the same Mug was responsible for the arrest of Balzac, and they could only deduce that
he was in fact working for the Germans. It was a worrying coin-
cidence; it was plausible that he had informed on the March 29
meeting.

That same day, the Gestapo broke down the door of the de
Prévaux's flat in rue Rossini in Nice. Lotka had just returned
from Lyon with the mail and money for the Anne sub-network.
They took her away. She had barely time to thrust her baby into
the arms of Nana, the nurse, and whisper: "Quick! Hide her!"
Aude, who was just nine months old, was dressed like a princess.
Lotka had spent a fortune on getting a couturiere from the
Faubourg Saint-Honoré to send her smocked dresses, prewar
crêpe de Chine chemisettes, and silk-lined bouclé lambswool
coats. Aude was taken to safety by Nana, whose name was
Joséphine Schweitzer, to her poor home in a working-class district of Nice. Lotka wrote to ask her not to part with the child on
any pretext. At first she was to keep her with her, and then in the
summer (Lotka was clear about the likely length of her deten-
tion), she should take her to the country—among other places to
Cabris to the Mayrisches, whose daughter Andrée Viénot might
perhaps take her in.

The faithful nurse looked after Aude for nine months, forgetting about her wages and getting by on the subsidies provided
by the network. In December she took the baby to Paris, to
Jacques' brother.

De Prévaux was at first held in the Prison des Baumettes in
Marseille. Lotka was moved from les Baumettes to l'Hermitage

in Nice to be interrogated—two days here, two days there, the idea being to disorient and exhaust her until she was completely demoralized. In les Baumettes they took her to see Jacques, hoping that one or the other would weaken on seeing in the other's face the only too evident traces of the torture undergone. In vain. Whether they were brought together for a so-called confrontation in the midst of the sneers and abuse of a cellarful of police, or passed each other by chance in the prison's gloomy corridors, Jacques caught Lotka's eye and held it. Lotka was riveted to Jacques' eyes, and just a moment was sufficient for each to assure the other of their strength, or to renew it. They straightened their shoulders and, heads held high, faced their torturers unbowed.

Later, in May or June, they were moved to the Fort de Montluc in Lyon, where Klaus Barbie reigned supreme. Lotka was not handed over to him on racial grounds, and this spared her immediate deportation or a horrifying execution. She was not, for instance, sent on the convoy of a hundred and twenty prisoners taken to the woods in Saint-Genis Laval at dawn on August 20, 1944, summarily shot in an abandoned house and then burned, dead or alive. Instead, F2's leaders were interrogated by a special Gestapo commando expressly sent from Berlin, and later directly by a captain of the Wehrmacht. The interrogations took place in a house requisitioned for the purpose.

The Gestapo's orders were to make Vox and Kalo talk at all costs. They knew they had got their hands on one of the five or six principal leaders of F2, the network that had been so injurious to German activities and until then impossible to liquidate. They had no doubt that if they went about it the right way, their hostages would eventually divulge names and addresses. Jacques (registered as number 6585) and Lotka (number 6575) were therefore—outside the interrogations, of course—treated with some respect, more like officers who were prisoners of war. They were kept in solitary confinement in their cells, whereas most of the prisoners were crammed into tiny rooms infested with vermin (which Jacques and Lotka didn't escape), with neither sanitation nor ventilation. On top of the normal rations of bread and soup, they were allowed a bit of meat from time to time. Finally, a privilege reserved for officers' wives, Lotka was able to wash their underwear. Toward the end, Jacques was given permission to smoke, a favor he owed to the fact that he had been a naval attaché in Berlin and had some acquaintances in common with the Wehrmacht captain interrogating him.

Jacques was kept in solitary confinement and only let out under close guard when he was to be interrogated. It was impossible for him to communicate with his fellow prisoners, but he managed to pass on a little information through Henri Stroweis, who had found a way to talk to him in the Gestapo cellars. His main concern, Stroweis later said, was that the network should continue to operate; he had instructions to give to certain sectors. It was also thanks to Stroweis's cunning and courage that Jacques received news of Lotka and his fellow prisoners.

Did he hear that the end of the war was in sight, that the Germans were retreating in Normandy, that on August 15 the Allies had landed triumphantly in Provence? This had been the object of all his efforts, the raison d'être for the meticulous and difficult work undertaken by Anne's agents. In all probability he never knew its outcome, although he may have guessed it from his SS guards' nervousness and the increased violence of his torturers. Alone, then, and deprived of any solidarity with his fellow combatants, he still found the inner strength to resist torture.

Lotka's cell, by contrast, was in the middle of a corridor, and her fellow prisoners could see her through their spy holes as she passed by with a wardress on her way to wash or to the ten minutes' allotted exercise, and sometimes even exchange a few words with her. In general, their aim was to pass on the rare news that managed to reach Montluc. Lotka did her best to convince the others that the day of their liberation was close and that they must hold out, never give in, and never talk. "Of course we won't," she assured them. "We won't be taken to Germany, we shall be liberated right here." She called out of her window into the courtyard: "Be patient, it won't be long. They're on their way!" This unshakeable optimism concealed her terrible anguish about the fate of her baby, of whom she had heard nothing. In addition she had to endure different forms of inhuman torture—by immersion, by electric shock, and others so degrading that she couldn't bring herself to speak of them to her companions, she was too ashamed. It was also torture to listen for the orders barked out at dawn, ever more frequently: "So-and-so, no belongings"—which everyone knew meant death—and then, her heart beating wildly, to listen for the next name, very possibly her own.

From mid-August, prisoners were massacred daily. Exasperated by the growing strength of the Resistance, panicked by the pressure of the Allied armies marching from both Normandy and Provence toward Lyon, the Gestapo headquarters in the Place Bellecour had begun a sinister "cleansing" operation aiming to eliminate all the unfortunate witnesses to their barbarity. Every night now, cellmates were taken away to an unknown destination. It occasionally happened that some were returned to the prison because there was no room for them on the trucks—a respite of a few hours—and they described the horrors. In this atmosphere of fear a mass was said on the 17th in the women's quarters. This was the first religious service celebrated in Montluc. All the women attended it, whether Catholic or not, with equal gravity, and trembled as they received collective absolution. Since the priest—a German—had no choirboy, he appealed for a volunteer among the faithful. Lotka offered her services. She, who had not been christened yet was a profound believer, served her first and last mass with intense emotion.

Two days later, at seven in the evening on August 19, 1944, the fatal order "no belongings" rang out in Montluc. Among the twenty-four resistants' names yelled out in the corridor—twenty men and four women—were those of Jacques and Lotka.

Lotka's first reaction was a cry of joy; she thought she was being liberated. But she soon realized that she was going to be executed. Surrounded by her three weeping companions, she remained dignified. As they left the buildings they were handed over to an SS formation, armed to the teeth, who amid a torrent of abuse beat them with their rifle butts and shoved them into a truck. They were taken to the airfield in Bron, ten kilometers from the center of Lyon. There, they were lined up in front of trenches—shell holes, in fact—and machine-gunned. Without anyone making sure that they were actually dead, their bodies were hastily covered with earth and rubble.

Four days later, the Gestapo abandoned the Fort de Montluc, and its survivors were liberated. On September 2, the German garrison withdrew from Lyon. On September 3, General de Lattre de Tassigny entered the liberated city.

Did Vox and Kalo speak under torture? They suffered agonies, but neither of them gave way. If they had given the Gestapo any information, it would have been enough to annihilate Anne and F2. To their comrades, they were heroes. Not only did Jacques manage not to compromise any of his chiefs or subordinates, he also took all the responsibility upon himself in order to mitigate the punishment those arrested with him might suffer.

All the prisoners who came into contact with Lotka were struck by her courage and dignity. "There were many conjectures made about her in the cells. Some said she was an American. Others said she was the wife of a leader of the Resistance. We all admired her dignity and apparent calm," one of them wrote. Another, speaking of "that beautiful young woman who comforted us by her courage and optimism," declared: "I saw many courageous women during the fifteen months I spent in German prisons, but I assure you that I never met a woman as brave and strong in spirit as Madame de Prévaux. . . . If the word 'heroine'—which she wouldn't have liked because she thought everything she did was perfectly natural—can be applied to anyone, it should certainly be applied to her." And yet another: "I remember her smile and her kindness. She was like an angel who had come to visit me in my distress."

AFTERWORD

The bodies of the 24 members of the Resistance executed on August 19, 1944, were exhumed from the mass grave in Bron immediately after the liberation of Lyon. The remains of Jacques and Lotka now rest in the Bron military cemetery.

When I discovered where they were buried, I went to visit their graves. My heart heavy, I had to search for a long time among the hundreds of indistinguishable wooden crosses until I found those under which my parents lay. As I got closer, I felt my courage failing and I dared not look for the names I was afraid of finding. I wished I hadn't come. I wanted to run away and forget it all.

Nevertheless I went back, and each time I had the same feeling of anger at the fact that they were lying there unknown, lost among those masses of identical graves. Death, of course, is the great equalizer, and there can be no distinction between heroes. But the dead live in the memory of the living, and no one—or almost no one—knew who Jacques and Lotka de Prévaux were, what they had done with their liberty, what passions had driven them or what courage had sustained their sacrifice.

In the eyes of the navy, my father had been wrong not to join the Free French in London—as if geographical proximity to de Gaulle were the only way to save the rebels who had defied their chief of staff, Darlan. For the Gaullists, he was merely one obscure resistant among thousands. Also, he was suspected of having preferred a Polish network to the Free French Intelligence Service (BCRA). There was no one to keep their memory alive. The Polish members of my family had been exterminated, and the Trolley de Prévaux had decided to forget this unusual episode in their family history. So Jacques and Lotka were consigned to oblivion.

Each time I went to the Bron military cemetery I became more and more aware of an inner voice telling me I could not let them die a second time.

So I decided to reconstitute their life and find the thread running through it. As it turned out, some people did know about parts of their lives: Jacques' military career, Lotka's childhood, her feminine friendships, Vox's role in the F2 network. . . . But these were just odds and ends. The essential thread that binds a human being and gives meaning to his life was missing.

For many years I did no more than entertain this pious intention, but I did go and see the members of the family who knew more. The scales having fallen from my eyes, I made the same journeys I had made as a child. I went to see my Belgian godmother, and my godfather Sliwinski, whom I had seen a few times in Paris as a child and with whom I had spent a happy holiday in Morocco when I was sixteen. I bitterly reproached him for having evaded the naïve questions I had asked him at the time. "Godfather, how did you come to know my parents?" (For me they were François and Micheline.) "Why did they choose you, when they never see you?" He told me, with tears in his eyes, that Micheline had made him promise never to tell me anything about my origins; if he hadn't, she wouldn't have let me go and stay with him.

But the raw material he revealed haphazardly to me was incomplete and one-sided. What was I to do with it? Being a journalist, I couldn't be satisfied with the account of just one witness. I took refuge behind the obvious material and methodological difficulties: I would have to find other witnesses, accu-

mulate documents, separate the true from the false, decide between different versions of the same story, elucidate enigmas,
justify or demolish rumors. For example, did Jacques join the
Resistance because he had married a Jewish woman, as the
Trolley de Prévaux family maintained? Did Lotka really work
for Vionnet, as the Leitners said? How could I know? After all,
I am not a historian. . . . This seemed a good enough reason to
retreat from the obstacle and let my research drag on indefi-
nitely.

Suddenly by pure chance, some documents of incalculable importance reached me. These were the love letters between
Jacques and Lotka: one part had been kept by Mathilde Pascalis, another by her son, Eric, and together they complemented
a third part I had in my possession. My father had made
Mathilde Pascalis swear that she would give the letters only to
his daughter, and this she could do only when we made contact,
which did not happen until 1994. The letters answered almost
all my remaining questions. I really did have to begin to fulfill
the duty I had imposed on myself in the presence of my parents' too-modest graves.

Nevertheless, when all the information had been sorted out,
the dossiers classified and a few chapters already drafted, one
last obstacle remained and held everything up. A gap in the biography of the characters, a shadowy area, a mystery—of minimum historical interest, no doubt, but for me it was vital. I still
didn't know how my parents had met, where and when Jacques
had made Lotka's acquaintance. Until I knew that, I would find
it impossible to write. Everyone I asked gave me casual an-
swers, as if the event were of no great importance. "They could
well have met in a tearoom, or even in the street. . . . There are
so many ways for a man to get to know a woman!"

Then, in one of Jacques' letters to Lotka I noticed the name
Crevel. By then I knew about Lotka's friendship with Mopse

JACQUES DE PRÉVAUX'S MILITARY CAREER

1888   April 4: Born in Paris.
        Ecole Saint-Joseph (Jesuit school in Lille).

1906   Admitted to the Naval College.

1908   Left the Naval College (fifth out of forty-eight).

1908—09 Training cruise around the world; midshipman on training ship *Duguay-Trouin.*

1910   Battleship *Charlemagne* in Toulon; attached to main armament and fire control teams.

1911   **October 5: Enseigne de vaisseau (Sublieutenant).**

1912—13 *January:* Cruiser second class *Descartes* (Newfoundland and east coast of America), attached to special section: electronics, torpedoes, fire precautions (until October 1913).

1913—14 In Toulon (until April 1914).

1914   *April:* First Fleet, torpedo flotilla. Second officer torpedo boat *Fanfare.*
        August: Navigating officer and gunnery officer on torpedo boat *Chasseur.*

1916   *May:* Assistant gunnery officer on the *Paris.*
        June: Second officer on gunboat *Diligente,* patrolling the eastern Mediterranean.

1917   *June to September:* Course at Saint-Cyr (Versailles) Naval Aviation center: airship pilot's license.
        August 2: Lieutenant de vaisseau (Lieutenant–Commander).

1917–20	*October:* First command: Marquise-Rinxent airship base, until November 1919: then Montebourg (Cotentin) base until February 1920.
1920	Aide-de-camp to the minister of the navy.
1922	*January:* Commander of the gunboat *Diligente,* and commander of the minesweeping flotilla of the Toulon fifth District, until January 1924.
1923	**July 25: Capitaine de corvette (Lieutenant–Commander).**
1924	*April–June:* Airship pilot's refresher course.
	June: Commander of Naval Aviation in Cuers-Pierrefeu until August 1926.
1925	*October:* Naval attaché in Berlin until January 1931.
1928	**January 17: Capitaine de frégate (Commander).**
1931	*May:* Commander of the sloop *Altaïr,* Far East naval forces, until July 1933.
1934	*June:* Commander of marine aviation base at Rochefort.
1935	*October to December:* Toulon.
	December: Staff College—"auditor" (*Centre des hautes études navales*).
1937	**August 1: Capitaine de vaisseau (Captain).**
	July to November: Toulon.
	November: Collège des hautes études de défense nationale, until April 1938.
1938	*August:* Command of the cruiser *Duguay-Trouin,* now a training ship attached to the Toulon gunnery school.
1939	Assigned to the French West African convoy and patrol division, then to the French squadron in the eastern Mediterranean.
1940	*May:* Force X in Alexandria.
	October: Repatriated to Toulon for health reasons.
	November: Extension of convalescent leave.

1941   *July:* Chairman of the Toulon Maritime Court.
         December: Extended leave.
1943   *April:* Retirement.
1944   *August 19:* Executed at Lyon-Bron.

PRINCIPAL DECORATIONS AND AWARDS

I. Jacques de Prévaux

1. Before 1939

Chevalier of the Legion of Honour, June 16, 1920: "has shown exceptional brilliance in his command of a vitally important airship center."

Officer of the Legion of Honor, January 21, 1931.

Croix de Guerre, November 14, 1918: "A valuable officer, who through his energy and enthusiasm obtained the maximum output from the Marquise airship center, under frequent air raids. Has many flying hours to his credit."

2. For Acts of Resistance

Distinguished Service Order, January 31, 1943.

Commander of the Legion of Honor, April 10, 1945: "A senior officer of outstanding merit and of the greatest patriotism. Was one of the first to rally to the cause of the Liberation. As commander of an intelligence network, regularly provided information of the greatest importance. Was in all circumstances distinguished by his remarkable qualities as a leader of men and his total disregard of danger. Arrested by the Germans, suffered both physical and mental torture without yielding. Was an admirable example to everyone of courage and the spirit of sacrifice." This decoration includes the award of the Croix de Guerre, with bar.

Virtuti Militari (a Polish decoration), April 19, 1945, for "remarkable acts of warfare on French territory during the German Occupation."

Croix de la Libération, January 18, 1946: "A senior officer of outstanding merit, endowed with the most admirable spirit of sacrifice. Joined the Resistance in 1941, and from then on devoted his entire life to the cause of the Liberation, taking command of an intelligence network which he led brilliantly until 29 March 1944, when he was arrested and tortured by the enemy. In all circumstances gave proof of the most complete disregard of danger, and was an admirable example to his men of patriotism and the spirit of sacrifice."*

3. Promotion

On April 16, 1945, de Prévaux was promoted to Rear Admiral, with a return to the active list dated from January 1, 1941, and the cancellation of his "suspension from the active list (*congé d'activité*)." This was therefore not a posthumous nomination, relatively easy to decide on, but a very real promotion. At the time it was decreed, in fact, de Prévaux was listed as "missing," since formal proof of his execution, and his death certificate, only dated from November 1945. "Given the importance of his services to his country and the admirable qualities of courage and devotion he has demonstrated, it is to be hoped that Captain Trolley de Prévaux, missing since his arrest, may be fittingly rewarded. . . . A proposal of promotion to the rank of Rear Admiral, backdated to come into effect on 1 January 1941, would

---

*Created by General de Gaulle, *L'Ordre de la Libération* consists of 1,038 "Companions." Only 238 crosses were awarded posthumously. (The list of Companions was closed in 1946.)

be fully justified." (Lieutenant Colonel Debesse, justificatory report to Admiral d'Argentieu.)

4. Justificatory Reports

Vincent Rozadowski (Pascal), head of network F2: "A naval officer of great merit who, when dismissed by Darlan in 1941, immediately sought the means of joining the Free French Forces. In November 1941, determined to serve at all costs, he got in touch with Foch, of network F2 and, despite the difference in rank, worked as a simple informer and provided excellent information on the enemy's navy.

"In the spring of 1942, the head of the network gave him the job of setting up an autonomous 'Naval' intelligence sector, which he then led. In the spring of 1943 after the fall of the F1 network, he showed extreme efficiency in helping to organize the 'Anne' (Mediterranean) sector of network F2, of which he became the head in April 1943.

"In his leadership of this network he demonstrated his remarkable organizational talents and total disregard of danger, and made sector 'Anne' the model for all other sectors. For a year he succeeded in having the whole Mediterranean coast covered by his informers and in providing the Allies with regular intelligence of the greatest importance (many telegrams of thanks, and the award of the DSO).

"An admirable leader of men, the strict discipline he imposed on them was based on mutual confidence, and he was liked and respected by all his subordinates. Despite his deteriorating health, he never allowed himself a moment's rest. With no thought for his career or promotion, he devoted himself to the very end to the leadership of the organization with which he had been entrusted.

"Arrested on 29 March 1944 and charged with being the head of an Allied intelligence network, he stoically suffered lengthy tortures without ever compromising anyone, claiming personal responsibility for everything. For everyone who worked with him, he was—and always will be—a model of loyalty, courage and disinterested patriotism."

Lieutenant Colonel Debesse, head of the Fighting France Service: "A senior officer of the greatest moral stature, as from 1941 he tried to find a way to join the forces of the Free French. Having made contact with an intelligence network, at the request of his chiefs and despite his high rank he continued to serve in France rather than going to England, considering that he would be of greater use in France. In spite of his age and rank, he began his work as a simple informer, and in this role he rendered remarkable services.

"He gradually came to take over the running of a very important intelligence network, and for more than a year regularly provided information of the greatest importance about the fleets and defensive organizations of the enemy in the Mediterranean. Throughout his command he gave proof of the most admirable disregard of danger and of total dedication to his task, despite its peril and his much impaired health. An admirable leader of men, he was able to impose perfect discipline on all his subordinates and was an example of patriotism and the spirit of sacrifice to all his agents.

"Arrested on 29 March 1944, he stoically suffered lengthy torture. Not only did he not give away anything about the organization he commanded, but he tried to assume all the responsibility and so make things easier for his men."

II. Lotka de Prévaux

The Cross of Valor (Polish decoration), September 12, 1942. *The Golden Cross of Merit, with bar* (Polish Decoration), April 13, 1945. *Médaille de la Résistance,* posthumously, May 5, 1945. Justificatory report: "When she first entered the network she acted as her husband's secretary but then, demanding more dangerous work, became an agent entrusted with special missions and a courier for the head of the network. In this capacity she accomplished several dangerous and important missions: liaising with the Americans, accompanying Allied soldiers, transporting mail. In all the missions she was given she showed extraordinary sangfroid, exemplary courage and remarkable tenacity. She always volunteered for the most difficult and dangerous missions. Arrested on 30 March 1944,* she underwent appalling tortures without betraying the important secret addresses she knew. Thus she saved her network's team leaders. She was shot in Bron on 19 August 1944."

Croix de la Libération. Strictly speaking, Lotka was not herself appointed a Companion of the Liberation. It is true that only six women were awarded the Croix de la Libération by the time the Order was closed in 1946. Nevertheless, she is considered by the Order to be one of their members. In the *Mémorial des Compagnons,* the entry relating to Admiral Jacques Trolley de Prévaux ends as follows:

"United in the action of resistance, united in the ordeal of prisons, they were once again united in their sacrifice. Therefore we in this Order shall not separate them under the Cross of Lorraine."

*Other independent witnesses give the date of Lotka's arrest as 29 March.

SOURCES

The information regarding Jacques de Prévaux's career and his superior officers' assessments comes from his personal file preserved in the Archives du Service Historique de la Marine, in Vincennes.

Jacques de Prévaux's correspondence and diaries, and from 1934 Lotka's letters, were an important source of information, as were quite a few military documents.

As the archives from the Service Historique de la Marine (SHM) have been used in almost every chapter, they will not be mentioned on each occasion. On the other hand, those from private collections (PC) are various as well as recurrent, and these will be mentioned at each instance.

PART I

1. The Would-be Buccaneer

Diary of the 1908–9 cruise on the training ship *Duguay-Trouin*. (PC)

Abbé Lebeurier, *Etat des anoblis (sic) en Normandie de 1645 à 1661;* Evreux, 1866.

P. de Longuemare, *Notes sur une descendance normande d'un frère de la Pucelle d'Orléans,* Caen, 1915.

2. The War Years

Letters from Jean Roulier and his mother to Jacques de Prévaux. (PC)

Gabriele D'Annunzio's oration at Jean Roulier's funeral. (PC)

Claude Farrère, *Fumée d'opium*, Editions Kailash, 1996.

La Patrie and *La Presse*, Montreal, July 10, 11 and 14, 1913; *Le Courrier de la Plata*, 12 March 1913.

Letters from Roland de Margerie to Jacques de Prévaux. (PC)

3. Airship Pilot

On the history of the Naval Air Service:

Vice Admiral Vercken, *Histoire succincte de l'aéronautique navale*, ARDHAN, 1993.

N. Desgouttes, *Les commandements des origines de l'Aéronautique navale*, ARDHAN, 1994.

C. V. Muracciole, *L'Aéronautique navale, des origines à 1918*, published by the Service Central de l'Aéronautique navale.

Commander de Brossard, *Lâchez tout!*, France-Empire, 1956.

4. Rank and Respectability

Letters to Jacques de Prévaux from Roland de Margerie and Catherine Ollivier.

General Order no. 46 from Jean de Laborde, commander of the air patrols of the Armies of the North. (PC)

L'Aéronautique navale de Cuers-Pierrefeu de 1917 à 1972, brochure published by the Division des constructions de l'Aéronautique navale de Toulon, 1972, and the works mentioned in chapter 3, above.

5. Naval Attaché in Berlin

On the historical context and the atmosphere in Berlin:

Benoist-Méchin, *Histoire de l'armée allemande,* Albin Michel, 1936.

G. Badia, *Histoire de l'Allemagne contemporaine,* Editions Sociales, 1964.

A. Bérard, *Au temps du danger allemand,* Plon, 1976.

Nicolas Sombart, *Jugend in Berlin,* Carl Hanser Verlag, Munich, 1983.

On René Crevel and Mopse:

M. Carassou, *René Crevel,* Fayard, 1989.

F. Buot, *René Crevel,* Grasset, 1991.

On Pierre and Andrée Viénot:

Dictionnaire biographique du mouvement ouvrier français, published by Jean Maitron, fourth part, 1993.

On the Franco-German Committee:

F. Lhuillier, *Dialogues franco-allemands 1925–1933,* published by the Faculty of Letters, University of Strasburg, 1971.

Pierre Viénot, *Incertitudes allemandes,* 1931 (translated as *Is Germany Finished?* Faber & Faber, London, 1931).

6. On the China Seas

On the historical context and the atmosphere in Shanghai:

André Malraux, *La Condition humaine*, 1933.

Guides to Shanghai.

Rapport sur la situation économique en Chine, presented to the 19 June 1931 General Assembly of the French Chamber of Commerce in China. (PC)

On the *Altaïr*'s itinerary:

Positions et mouvements de l'Altaïr, 1930–33, Marine Archives, Brest.

Shanghai diary, 24 April 1932.

On the Sino-Japanese incidents in Shanghai in January 1932:

Collection of operation orders.

Telegrams addressed by the Supreme Commander in the Shanghai Roads to the Vice Admiral Commander in Chief of Naval Forces in the Far East.

Collection of daily information bulletins of the Political Division of the police. (All PC)

On Blandine and Fascism:

Blandine Ollivier, *Jeunesse fasciste*, Gallimard, 1934.

L'Allemagne et nous, Le Document, January 1939. (PC)

PART II

7. From Jaroslaw to Vionnet; and 8. Conquest by Correspondence

On Jaroslaw and the Leitner family:

Testimony of Willy Leitner to the author.

On Mopse:

Letters from Mopse to Lotka. (PC)

René Crevel, *Lettres de désir et de suffrance*, Fayard, 1997.

Lettres à Mopse, edited by M. Carassou, Paris-Méditerranée, 1997.

On Vionnet:

J. Demornex, *Madeleine Vionnet*, Éditions du Regard, 1990. (translated as *Madeleine Vionnet*, Thames & Hudson, London, 1991).

Madeleine Chapsal, *La Chair de la robe*, Fayard, 1989.

Testimony of Natacha Duché to the author.

9. Rochefort

On the Rochefort Naval Air Base:

The works mentioned in Part I, chapter 3.

70 ans d'Aéronautique navale à Rochefort, published by the BAN in 1986.

Les dirigeables de Rochefort, Cols bleus review, 13 October 1984.

Testimony from Admiral de Brossard and Camille Migaud to the author.

Testimony from Daniéla Jeanson.

10. A Double Life

Leitner and Trolley de Prévaux family letters. (PC)

Letters to Jacques de Prévaux from Pierre Viénot and F. Piétri. (PC)
On the CHEN: SHM archives:

Testimony of Natacha Duché to the author.

Dossier of Maître Lesourd (divorce proceedings). (PC)

11. On the Duguay-Trouin

J. Guilini and A. Moreau, *Les Croiseurs de 8,000 T,* Marines Editions, 1995.

Accounts of the activity of the *Duguay-Trouin* from August 25, 1939, to June 22, 1940. (PC)

Georges Debat, *Marine oblige,* Flammarion, 1974.

Letters from Georges Debat to Jacques de Prévaux.

Testimony of Georges Debat and Guy Simon to the author.

12. Force X in Alexandria

The works, letters and testimony mentioned in the preceding chapter.

E. de Larminat, *Chroniques irrévérencieuses,* Plon, 1952.

Bertrand, *Les Forces navales françaises libres,* Argout, 1980.

V. A. Chaline and C.V. Santarelli, *Historique des FNFL,* SHM, 1989.

J. L. Crémieux-Brilhac, *La France libre,* Gallimard, 1996.

Communications and orders from the general staff of Force X and from the commander of the *Duguay-Trouin.* (PC)

PART III

The information about the F2 Network comes from various sources:

V. Masson, *La Résistance dans le Var,* l'Association des MUR du Var, 1983.

J. M. Guillon, *Le Var, la guerre, la Résistance.* (PC)

"Le réseau F2," *Revue historique de l'armée,* 1952.

L. Sliwinski, *Historique du réseau F2,* 1976. (PC)

Various authors, *Le Réseau Azur,* 1977. (PC)

L. Sliwinski and T. Jekiel, "Les services de renseignements polonais pendant la Seconde Guerre mondiale," communication, 9 November 1984. (PC)

L. Sliwinski, "La Résistance et le renseignement dans la Seconde Guerre mondiale," communication, March 1984.

T. Wyrwa, "La résistance polonaise en France," in *Revue d'histoire de la Seconde Guerre mondiale,* PUF, April 1986.

G. Havard, "Mes souvenirs de guerre." (PC)

J. L. Crémieux-Brilhac, *op. cit.*

H. Noguères, *Histoire de la résistance en France,* Robert Laffont, 1976; II, III, IV.

——*La vie quotidienne des résistants de l'armistice à la Libération,* Hachette, 1984.

J. P. Azéma, *De Munich à la Libération,* Le Seuil, 1979 (translated as *From Munich to Liberation,* CUP, 1984).

D. Veillon, *Le Franc-Tireur,* Flammarion, 1977.

Hinsley, *British Intelligence in the Second World War,* London, H.M.S.O., 1979.

National Archives.

Testimony given to the author by L. Sliwinski, G. Havard, J. Lévy-Rueff, Stanislas Lucki, Pierre Fourcaud, Mathilde Pascalis, Admiral de Lachadenède, and Eva Bringué-Tournier.

Unfortunately, the archives of the Second Bureau of the Polish Admiralty are missing. According to L. Sliwinski, those entrusted to their leader, Lieutenant-Colonel Langenfeld, disappeared; others were probably burned in July 1945, and it is not permitted to consult those that were transmitted to the British secret services.

13. In the Maritime Court

On Jacques de Prévaux's "suspension from active duty":

Bulletin of the Club for former members of the National Defense Special services, 3rd quarter, 1989.

Letters and testimony from Colonel Paillole to the author.

Order for extended leave, law of 8 November 1941, establishing the position of suspension from active duty. (PC)

SHM archives.

14. Commitment; and 15. F2—A Franco-Polish Network

Letter from Auguste-Henry Brun. (PC)

Testimony from J. Lévy-Rueff and G. Havard. (National Archives)

16. The Subterfuge

On the Sliwinski/de Prévaux meeting:

Account by L. Sliwinski and written testimony from Tadeusz Korycki (Bey).

On the links between F2 and the British Intelligence services and relations with the FFL or the BCRA:

The already-mentioned works by Crémieux-Brilhac, Noguères and Hinsley.

Jacques de Prévaux's file in the Polish Second Bureau in London. (PC)

Letter from L. Sliwinski to Pierre T. de P.

Testimony from J. Lévy-Rueff.

Letter from Jacques de Prévaux to Pierre Viénot. (PC)

17. A Simple Informer

Testimony from Mathilde Pascalis, Pierre Fourcaud, Raymond Leibovici. (The last: National Archives)

Statutes of the SPAM. (PC)

18. Fighting in the Shadows

H. Noguères, *Le suicide de la Flotte française à Toulon,* Laffont, 1961.

On the DSO:

List of French sailors awarded the DSO (letter from the British admiralty, PC). The accompanying citation has disappeared, as Jacques de Prévaux's file was destroyed. "It was impossible to keep all the Second World war files," the Admiralty wrote to me.

The quotation from de Lattre de Tassigny has been taken from the work by Masson (*op. cit.*).

19. The Arrest of the Leitners

Letters from Bertha and Isidore Leitner, Jeanne Leitner and Mme. Lelong. (PC)

21. Montluc

Written testimony from Henri Stroweis (Balzac), Mlle. Mortorel, Dolly Argaud, Mme. Vasteenberghe, Ginette, Guilon de Langeron, Captain Gout, Marcelle Trillat. (PC)

Plan of the Bron mass grave, death certificates. (PC)

Account of the Bron and Saint-Genis-Laval killings, in *La Marseillaise,* September 11, 12, 13 and 14, 1944, and *France-Soir,* September 3, 1984.

ABOUT THE AUTHOR

Aude Yung–de Prévaux was the Geneva correspondent of the daily newspaper *Libération*, and also contributed to a number of French and Swiss publications. In 1999 she was awarded the Prix Saint-Simon and the Prix Maréchal Foch de l'Académie Française for the original French edition of this book. She lives in Munich.

Barbara Wright is the distinguished translator of plays by Jean Genet, Eugène Ionesco and Samuel Beckett, and fiction by Raymond Queneau, Nathalie Sarraute and Jean Rouaud.